# Montessori Method

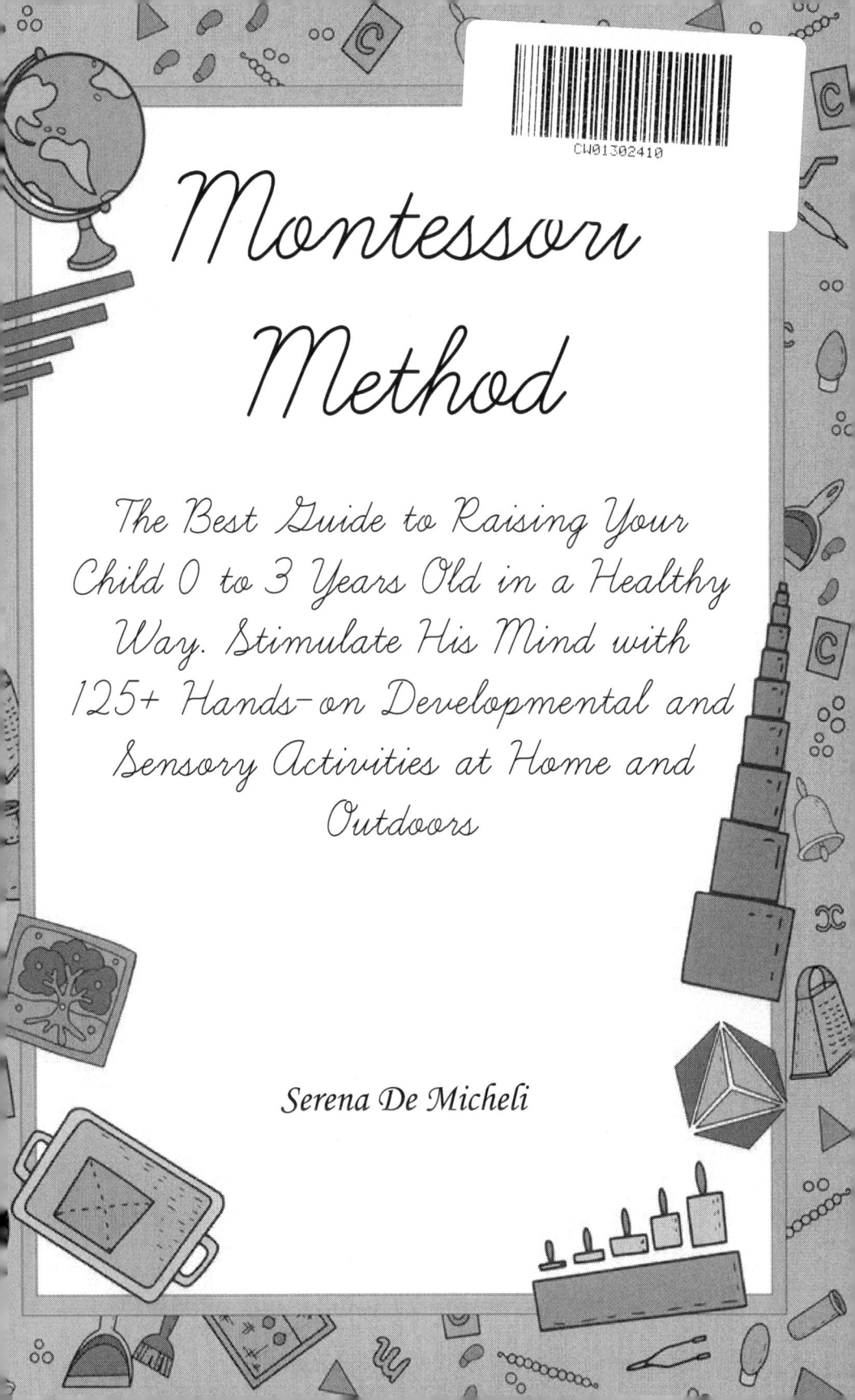

*The Best Guide to Raising Your Child 0 to 3 Years Old in a Healthy Way. Stimulate His Mind with 125+ Hands-on Developmental and Sensory Activities at Home and Outdoors*

Serena De Micheli

**Copyright - 2023 - Serena De Micheli**

**All rights reserved.**

The contents of this book may not be reproduced, duplicated, or transmitted without the written permission of the author or publisher. Under no circumstances shall the publisher, or the author, be held liable or legally responsible for any damages, compensation, or monetary loss due to the information contained in this book. Either directly or indirectly.

**Legal notice:**

This book is copyrighted. This book is for personal use only. You may not modify, distribute, sell, use, quote from, or paraphrase any part or content of this book without the consent of the author or publisher.

**Notice of disclaimer:**

Please note that the information contained in this document is for educational and entertainment purposes only. All efforts have been made to present accurate, current, reliable, and complete information. No warranty of any kind is stated or implied. Readers acknowledge that the author does not commit to provide legal, financial, medical, or professional advice. The contents of this book have been derived from various sources. Please consult a licensed professional before attempting any of the techniques described in this book.

By reading this document, the reader agrees that under no circumstances shall the author be liable for any losses, direct or indirect, incurred as a result of the use of the information contained in this document, including, but not limited to, - errors, omissions, or inaccuracies.

## Summary

**Introduction** ------ 6

**CHAPTER 1: Who Maria Montessori Was** ------ 8

*Maria Montessori and the Birth of Her Method* ------ 8

*Spreading the Montessori Method* ------ 11

*Why the Montessori Method Is Not an Integral Part of Italian Schools* ------ 12

**CHAPTER 2: The Montessori Method** ------ 14

*What Is the Montessori Method* ------ 14

*The Principles Underlying the Method* ------ 16

*How a Montessori School Works* ------ 25

*Abolition of Toys* ------ 27

*Role of the Teacher* ------ 27

*Scientific Evidence of the Method on Children* ------ 28

**CHAPTER 3: The Development of the Child from 0 to 3 Years of Age** ------ 30

*The Sensitive Periods* ------ 31

*Stages of Development* ------ 35

**CHAPTER 4: The Needs of the 0 to 3-Year-Old Child** ------ 41

*The Need for Direct Contact with the Mother* ------ 42

*The Need to Feel Protected and Safe* ------ 43

*The Need to Develop Relationships* ------ 43

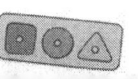

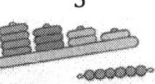

*The Need to Find Stable Landmarks* ------ 44

*The Need for His Biological Rhythms to be Respected* ------ 45

*The Need for Self-Awareness as an Individual* ------ 46

*The Need for Freedom and Independence* --- 47

*The Need for a Tailor-made Space* --- 48

*The Need for Concentration* --- 49

*The Need to Use Hands* --- 51

*The Need to Experience Nature* --- 53

*The Need for Silence* --- 53

**CHAPTER 5: The Role of the Parent** --- 55

*Treat Your Child with Respect* --- 56

*Meet His Needs* --- 56

*Follow His Interests* --- 56

*Communicate and Involve Him* --- 57

*Use Positive Discipline* --- 57

*Allow Them to Try New Experiences* --- 58

*Do Not Interrupt the Flow of Concentration* --- 59

*Propose Choices for Them* --- 59

*Limit the Number of Games Available to Him* --- 59

*Encourage but Do Not Reward* --- 60

*Always Tell Them the Truth* --- 60

*Turn off the TV* --- 61

**CHAPTER 6: Organizing the Home According to the Montessori Method** --- 62

*5 Tips for Organizing Your Home in the Montessori Style* --- 63

*The Nursery* --- 65

*Living Room* --- 70

*Kitchen* --- 70

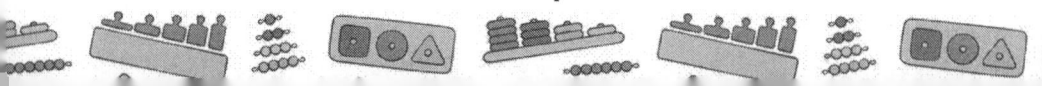

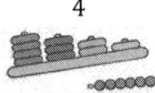

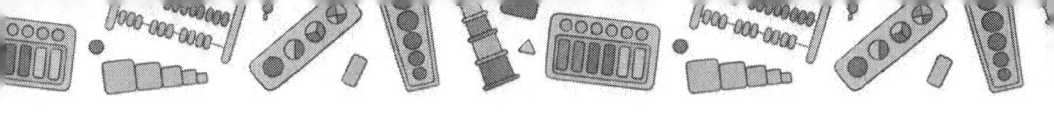

*Bathroom* ---------- *71*

## Chapter 7: Montessori Activities in the Home. — 73

*Stimulation Activities* ---------- *73*

*Practical Life* ---------- *90*

*Sensory Activities* ---------- *106*

*Development Activities* ---------- *123*

## Chapter 8: Montessori Outdoor Activities — 136

## Chapter 9: Recipes for the Youngest — 150

*Reasons to Involve Your Toddler in the Kitchen* ---------- *150*

*Tools* ---------- *151*

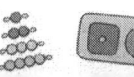

## Conclusions — 186

## Bibliography — 189

## Sitography — 189

# Introduction

If you have this book in your hands because you have probably heard of the Montessori Method, and it has been described to you as revolutionary concerning early childhood education.

But what does this method consist of? What benefits will you have from applying it to your child's growth and education? Is there scientific evidence to show that the Montessori Method is the best educational method ever? What Montessori activities can you offer your little one to help him develop his skills?

This book will help you learn about the Montessori Method in all its aspects and perform practical activities with your child, creating favorable conditions that stimulate him to bring out the best in him so he can develop his full potential. The book is divided into two parts:

- The first part will explain who Maria Montessori is, what her method consists of, why this method was revolutionary in the past, and why it is still revolutionary today; it will also examine the developmental stages of children from 0 to 3 years old, their needs at different stages of growth and what is the role of parents during this process;
- The second part will apply the principles of the Montessori Method practically through more than 125 indoor and outdoor activities and more than 30 recipes that will help you stimulate your child's mind and accompany him in his growth and development by making him increasingly independent and autonomous.

We conclude this brief introduction with the words of Maria Montessori, who guided us in creating this practical and effective guide for all new mothers and fathers who are looking for stimulation for their children:

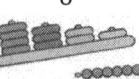

*"The child has its laws of development, and if we wish to help it grow, we must follow it, not already impose ourselves on it."* [1]

Happy Reading!

---

[1] M. MONTESSORI, *La mente del bambino,* Garzanti, Milan, 1952, 161.

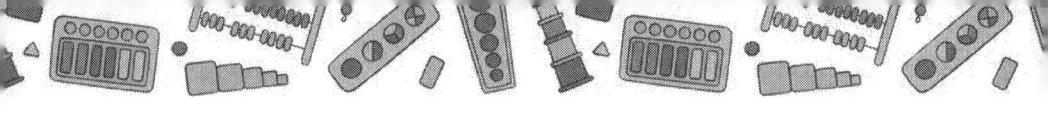

# Part I: The Montessori Method

## Chapter 1: Who Maria Montessori Was

*This is our mission: to cast a ray of light and pass on.*

*Maria Montessori*

### Maria Montessori and the Birth of Her Method

Maria Tecla Artemisia Montessori was born in Chiaravalle on August 31, 1870. She was an Italian educator, pedagogue, philosopher, physician, child neuropsychiatrist, and scientist. As one of the first women to graduate in medicine in Italy, she faced much prejudice from the scientific community, which at that time consisted only of men; this tenacity of hers led her to be very active in the feminist movements of the time.

In 1903 she was appointed Assistant Physician Class II on the rolls of the Executive Staff of the Italian Red Cross available for the services of Territorial Hospitals. Her career in school education began in 1904, soon after she obtained her free professorship in anthropology, which allowed her to deal with the educational organization of kindergartens.

In Rome, Montessori became aware of the social problems that led people to leave their children in a state of degradation or to abandon them. Maria's interests then shifted from social medicine to treating mental disorders to treating "dysfluent children", that is, children with a reduced capacity for interaction with the social environment compared to what is considered the norm. In those days, it was enough for children to be poor and left to their own devices for them to be placed in an institution for the mentally disturbed. A child left in a state of degradation often failed to develop their abilities and character like other children; therefore, if they had social or learning disorders, they were termed a "dysfluent child" and confined to a foster home, and it was considered impossible to educate them.

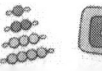

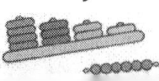

Maria Montessori became interested in these children and studied their behavior greatly, realizing that the little ones needed to do and establish contact with the world to develop their bodies and minds. Thus, their problem was not medical but pedagogical. Those children were excluded due to social, environmental, and historical causes, mainly due to poor living conditions, precarious hygienic situations, and families that were poor both materially and mentally. Proletarian class exploitation, adult ignorance, and illiteracy were other factors that fostered the physical and moral degeneration of very normal children. Maria realized that a dirty, sick, hungry, and exploited child was a reflection of the family this person belonged, which reflected the same characteristics; therefore, she decided to introduce those children left to their own devices into an environment that would stimulate them and could provide them with the necessary tools to develop both physically and mentally. Thus was born her Method: an educational practice through which the dysfluent child, subjected to continuous stimulation, could perform manual and intellectual work and acquire vocational skills that would make the child a useful member of society. The children followed by Maria Montessori were able to take the state exam along with their "normal" peers; they were subjected, just like the others, to tests in reading, writing, and arithmetic, and some of them turned out to be even better than the so-called "normal children" in public school[2].

In 1897, at a National Congress of Medicine held in Turin, Maria Montessori launched her first explicit accusation against society and the economic, political, and moral structures, which did not care for poor children and immediately classified them as "retarded" and "disturbed" without giving them any help and assistance. Society did not recognize the possibility of realizing oneself through one's abilities as a fundamental right of the individual. Maria's goal was to change society by helping children with mental difficulties, and she believed this was possible by developing an educational method based on scientific principles. Her interest was not limited to marginalized children but went far beyond that; in fact, she tried to understand why "normal" children in public schools remained on such a low learning level that they were matched on intelligence tests by children who, at that time and under those social conditions, were considered "non-normal." She understood that a radical change in education was needed and that this change could lead to a transformation of society. Thus it was that Maria Montessori, observing direct work in classrooms, began to develop a **scientific pedagogy** that was based first and foremost on taking care of the children's complexity, keeping in mind the different factors that influence them, such as the social context in which they live, physical health, and social conditions.

In 1907 Barons Alice and Leopoldo Franchetti helped open the first Children's Home in Rome. It was only a few years later that Maria, urged on by the Franchetti family, put in writing the first edition of her famous Method: *The Method of Scientific Pedagogy Applied to Children's Education in Children's Homes* (Città di Castello, Scipione Lapi, 1909), dedicating the work to her husband and wife. At the same time, she also held the first training course for

---

[2] *At that time, children with learning disabilities were considered "not normal" because they were different from those attending public school.*

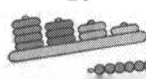

teachers on the Montessori Method in Città di Castello. Following this course, Baroness Franchetti opened a "Children's House" at Villa Montesca.

Among the first emerging figures in society to adopt the Montessori Method for their children's education was marquise Romeyne; her three children served as "guinea pigs" to test the Montessori materials experimented on at Villa Montesca in the summer of 1909. In the early fall of that year, the marquise decided to use the Montessori Method not only in teaching the Pischiello rural elementary school in Umbria but also to make up for the severe cultural backwardness of local childhood.

Maria Montessori traveled the world to spread her educational theory. She was forced to leave Italy for political reasons and had her greatest success in the United States; in 1913, the New York Tribune featured Maria Montessori as *the* most interesting woman in Europe. From then on, her method garnered considerable interest in North America. During her trip to India, the Montessori movement was born from which the "Montessori Teacher's School" and the "Opera Nazionale Montessori" would originate in 1924; the latter was aimed at the knowledge, dissemination, implementation, and protection of her method.

## *Spreading the Montessori Method*

World travel enabled Maria Montessori to export her method to many countries, including the United States, Germany, Holland, and India. But what are the reasons why her method was appreciated and spread abroad?

In the previous paragraph, we mentioned how rigid schooling was in those days; in a society with no respect for the small and helpless and no dignity was given to them, offering child-sized desks and materials was a great revolution. Perhaps today, accustomed to these kinds of objects, we do not reflect enough on how important these aids are for the growth and development of a child's mind. Additionally, the Montessori Method brought absolute innovations to how children are educated. Some reasons for its success are:

- **Scientificity:** it is a scientific method based on careful observation of children. No one before had studied children, their behaviors, and needs scientifically, nor had they created materials and objects suitable for them;
- **The innovative ideas:** such as educating teachers not to grade children, not to judge or punish them;
- **Educating for freedom:** children had the freedom to move and act spontaneously (which was impossible before then); they could take and use the materials they wanted and then put them back in their proper places;
- **All child-friendly:** children were free to move about the space and use materials of the right size for their small hands; desks were not arranged in fixed positions but were light enough for them to move them according to their preferences.

There are currently more than 22 thousand schools in the world based on the Montessori Method (66 thousand counting Montessori-directed schools where the main foundations of this educational method are applied anyway). Although it is a method that originated in Italy, there are little more than 140 recognized Montessori schools in our country, and in particular, there are Montessori kindergartens; as for the elementary school segment, it is very difficult to find schools that apply this method. On the other hand, Montessori schools have become very widespread, particularly in America, England, Germany, India, and Saudi Arabia.

## *Why the Montessori Method Is Not an Integral Part of Italian Schools*

Despite being successfully embraced and adopted by thousands of schools worldwide, the Montessori Method failed to grow and develop in Italy. It was partly due to Fascism, which held back the adoption of Maria Montessori's method, as she was forced to flee Italy in 1934; this was compounded by the traditional national conservatism that opposed her educational method, which was considered too costly because it would have required the state to invest a great deal of capital in changing teaching methods and training new teachers. Adopting the Montessori Method in Italian schools also meant laying off many of the school staff (since there were no face-to-face classes, one educator could follow a class with 50 children). Cutting teachers would consequently save a lot of money that could be used to purchase the materials needed for Montessori schools. Unfortunately, Maria's ideas were frowned upon by the majority, which is why even today in Italy, the Montessori Method has not been adopted in schools, but the old state method of face-to-face teaching is used.

Even today, public schools barely survive and do not have sufficient funds to renovate classrooms and provide specific teaching materials for this method. Despite this, many parents want to educate their children according to the Montessori Method, which is producing a significant increase in private Montessori schools, especially in Lombardy, Marche, Lazio, and Puglia.

To promote the development, study, and research of the Montessori Method nationally and internationally, the Opera Nazionale Montessori was founded in Italy. This association supports public and private Montessori schools to help develop "Children's Homes." Although it still seems like a utopia, we hope that soon our country will be able to apply this extraordinary teaching method in all schools nationwide.

We have seen in broad outline how the Montessori Method came about. Now we will look specifically at what it is and what its core principles are.

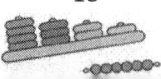

# Chapter 2: The Montessori Method

## What Is the Montessori Method

Talking about science education, in the book "*La scoperta del bambino*" *(The Discovery of the Child)*, Mary explains:

*"A science of education has not only the task of 'observing,' but also of 'transforming' children."* [3]

This kind of education was meant to "modify" and "improve" the individual because it was based on science. Montessori clearly explains that her method is based on **careful observation of** the individual child and the **preserving children's freedom** in spontaneous manifestations.[4] Thus, the basis of her educational method is freedom, and the teacher's task is to help the child

---

[3] M. MONTESSORI, *La scoperta del bambino*, Garzanti, Milan, 1970, 33.
[4] M. MONTESSORI *Il Metodo della Pedagogia Scientifica applicato all'educazione infantile nelle Case dei Bambini*, Edizioni Opera Nazionale Montessori, Rome, 2000.

conquer it. But why speak precisely of Method? Mary herself, in her book *Formation of Man* answers:

> "if we were to abolish not only the name but also the common concept of "method" and replace it with another indication, if we were to speak of an "aid so that the human personality may conquer its independence, of a means of freeing it from the oppression of ancient prejudices about education," then everything would become clear. It is the human personality and not a method of education that must be considered: it is the defense of the child, the scientific recognition of his nature, and the social proclamation of his rights that must replace the broken ways of conceiving 'education.'" [5]

In the early twentieth century, schools were modeled after the society of the time, which was highly capitalist. The discipline enforced in schools was rigid and cruel, aimed at preparing children for the world; they had to be obedient and conform to the masses, just as society wanted. They were forced into desks from which they could not move, and teaching was given to them in a rote learning teaching; how the school was set up repressed children's actions, creativity, and desire to discover and prevented them from making choices. Those who did not adhere to the pedagogical goals were discarded and confined to the reception centers, where they spent their days doing nothing. In a society where children were reviled and humiliated by adults, Maria's goal was to give them dignity by treating them with respect.

---

[5] M. MONTESSORI, *Formazione dell'uomo*, Garzanti, Milan, 1949, 11.

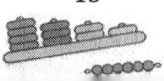

The method devised by Maria Montessori is proposed as an alternative to the rigorous education of the time and places the child at the center of everything, respecting and valuing their spontaneity and leading them to gain independence. Giving children dignity and treating them with respect allows them to have greater self-esteem and to discover and learn through their own mistakes; as a result, children acquire problem-solving skills and gain the independence they need to be prepared for adult life.

Adults must observe children and learn from them without disturbing their process of self-learning and self-correction. Their task is to defend their rights, especially the right to freedom.

In this chapter, we will look at the principles behind the Montessori Method, how a Montessori school is organized, what has been abolished, what is the role of teachers and adults, and the scientific evidence in children educated by this method. Let us begin our discussion by starting with the basic principles.

## The Principles Underlying the Method

### Freedom

The cardinal principle of the Montessori method is to **educate for freedom.** Associating the word freedom with children may make one think of a lack of education and limits; in reality, in a society where children were forced into silence and where their creativity was suppressed, a free child was a child who was free to move, to express himself, to be independent and to give vent to his notion. Freedom enables proper learning and healthy growth and development.

Children have an innate drive to know and act in the world, which leads them to choose and decide what activities to learn. Their innate curiosity is a real drive that enables them to learn spontaneously without outside influences or impositions. Speaking of the principle of freedom, Montessori explains:

> "When we, therefore, speak of a child's 'freedom,' we do not mean to consider the disordered external actions that children left to themselves would perform as an outburst of purposeless activity, but give the word the profound sense of the 'liberation' of his or her life from obstacles that impede its normal development."[6]

The method studied by Mary thus consists of leaving the child **free to act and develop his abilities,** respecting his own time and the ways he feels are best for his learning. This educational method allows him to explore the world by "doing" and fully develop his intelligence. To be helped in this process of growth and learning, he must live in an environment where stimuli suitable for his level of growth are present. In this regard, the environments, buildings, and teaching tools in Montessori schools are all "child-friendly," designed and developed to facilitate learning through self-correction of error.

Inside those walls, the little one is at home and can move from his classroom to the practical life classroom or to the environment he prefers and freely choose the activities he wants to engage in. This freedom, however, is not synonymous with confusion but with responsibility; in fact, the day is marked by fixed appointments that he learns to respect, such as work, free play, lunch, etc. We can therefore speak of a system of **"organized freedom"** understood as a condition that helps foster the child's physical and psychological development. The adult can facilitate this growth process by respecting it and offering the little one the help he needs to conquer his autonomy and form his personality.

---

[6] M.Montessori, *La scoperta del bambino*, Garzanti, Milan, 1970, 67.

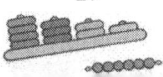

## Absorbing Mind

In analyzing their reactions when faced with proposed activities, Maria realized that in the first 3 years of life, toddlers are "absorbent sponges"; this means that all the impressions the toddler receives from the external environment are absorbed by his mind very naturally and without any effort. His learning takes place so unconsciously that he can learn passively, without engaging in concrete activity; he only needs to relate to the environment and his surroundings to grasp notions and make movements, behaviors, techniques, and activities his own. From this, it follows that **observation** is the best tool for acquiring whatever skills the toddler wants to develop.

After carefully observing, the toddlers try to imitate what they see peers and adults do. Thus, **imitation** is the second stage of learning, and real skill development takes place through it.

The third stage of learning is the **repetition of the exercise**; the latter may be unnecessary, tedious, and unrewarding for an adult, but for the toddler, it is the high road to learning because he performs a certain action until it succeeds him perfectly. The diagram below summarizes the three progressive stages of learning.

*observation* → *imitation* → *repetition*

## Customized Environment

Maria Montessori attached special importance to the beauty of the classroom. Learning materials had to be well made and well maintained, and objects had to be always in order on the shelves. Everything was created of a size within reach of children and of a weight that allowed them to maneuver the objects.

Maria's main change in school furniture was the abolition of desks. She had little tables and chairs built that were very light but not subject to shaking, so the children could move them as they pleased. The furniture was without dowels, grooves, and arches, so the little ones could clean them and keep them tidy. They also had wooden armchairs with wide arms and wicker chairs. Of course, everything was very colorful to give them a positive experience and make them feel comfortable.

The furnishings of the Children's House included a very low sink (accessible to a 3-year-old) with white, washable side shelves so that soaps, toothbrushes, towels, and a spittoon could be arranged. The sideboards were low and long to include many doors, each with a different lock and key. The sideboard also had a long, narrow top on which a placemat of linens was arranged; on the latter were placed in a lined-up fashion small flowerpots or a birdcage or a bowl with live fish to bring children closer to nature.

On the lower part of the walls were chalkboards and small boxes containing chalk and erasers. Above the blackboards hung pictures depicting children, animals, or family scenes.

"Suitable environment" means that all furnishings are child-friendly and the classroom's pace is calm and orderly. The Montessori environment houses true "corners" of activities such as:

- Corner of the activities of practical life;
- Language enrichment zone;
- Corner for listening to music;
- Symbolic play corner;
- Water room, manipulative and graphic-painting activities;
- Corner of the decants with granular substances and water;
- Corner of the sensory and developmental material.

Other important corners from an educational point of view are the meal, sleeping, and hygiene care environments.

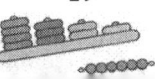

All spaces within the Children's House are designed, constructed, and prepared with objects and furnishings proportionate to children's age, physique, abilities, and motor needs so that children can actively use them until mastering them.

The environment should also be neat, organized, welcoming, calm, and warm. All these accouterments will enable the little ones to have stable and recognizable reference points and facilitate the expansion of their interests and experiences.

## Materials

The learning materials designed by Mary are structured in such a way as to learn without the need for an outside teacher but only by **self-experimentation** in which the learning materials themselves confirm the success or failure of the activity performed. The objects are not unbreakable but real: they are only lighter and smaller so that with little hands they can get a firm grip on them, and the risk of dropping them decreases; otherwise, they are like those of adults: the plates are ceramic, the glasses and jugs are glass, and the iron warms.

Montessori materials are not supportive but **developmental**; each material has a specific educational goal and allows the child to start from **sensory** (touch, smell, sight, and hearing) to lead to abstraction (abstract learning).

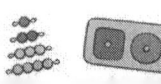

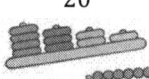

It is easy to find many materials on the Web that present the Montessori label but are not Montessori. Many materials, games, activities, and furnishings are mistakenly attributed to Maria Montessori just because they are made of wood or because they resemble or resemble the scientific materials she designed. It is precisely why clarity on the subject is necessary. In her texts, Maria Montessori describes some of her science materials in minute detail identifying their characteristics, what they look like, what they are used for, and how to use them. Then there are other materials that, even though they were not invented by Maria, can still be called **"Montessori-inspired" as** long as they meet the following characteristics:

- Must be of high quality;
- Have an aesthetic order;
- Must isolate one quality to allow the child to focus only on that one quality without getting confused;
- Must educate in self-correction of error;
- if it presents images, these must be scientifically accurate.

Montessori materials spark interest in the child and promote concentration and learning. For this reason, they must be not only beautiful but also appropriate, that they respect the characteristics above, and that they be orderly, clean, intact, and "intelligent".

## Learning to Move

Children get frustrated when they cannot do a movement perfectly. For this reason, more complex movements need to be broken down into simpler ones that can be learned perfectly. This way, they will repeat the same exercise until they can master a particular movement perfectly.

The old educational method demanded stillness and silence from the child; desks were fixed to the floor with nails, preventing the child from moving gracefully. In contrast, the tables and chairs created by Maria are light and transportable to allow the child to choose where to stand and sit (instead of sitting in place) with complete freedom. If during his movements the child bumps into desks or chairs or drops objects, this gives him **evidence of inability** and, at the same time, a chance to **self-correct by controlling the mistake**; if the chairs and tables remain still without producing noise, it means that the child *has learned to move*.

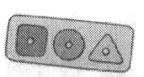

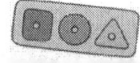

Referring to children's need to repeat an exercise until they reach perfection, Mary wrote:

*"Later it became clear that **every** exercise in movement, **any error** of which **can be controlled**, as in this case noise in silence, guides children to perfect it: the repetition of the exercise can lead anyone to an outward education of acts, so fine, that it would be impossible to obtain it by external teaching."* [7]

## The Silence

Silence does not mean the traditional silence required in schools so as not to disturb the lesson, but it is an achievement of the child and is the result of considerable effort.

At certain times of the day, Maria invited the children to avoid any sound, and slowly a stage of absolute silence was reached in the classroom, which allowed a whole series of sounds that generally went unnoticed while they were engaged in their exercises (the pelting of rain, the chirping of birds, the noise produced by the wind, etc.) to be highlighted. Silence is thus an activity and not a lack of activity: it is an achievement of the children that allow them to develop psychic and cognitive abilities such as that reflection, concentration, and understanding.

## Autonomy and Independence

Today many people think that to help a child, it is necessary to facilitate them by removing the obstacles in front of them and serving them in every way. By

---

[7] M. MONTESSORI, *Il segreto dell'infanzia*, Garzanti, Milan, 1950,169.

nature, every living wants to achieve independence through continuous activity, and this is also true for the child: he too wants to gain his freedom and does so with continuous effort through work. The child's instinct is to act alone without the help of others, and he tries to defend himself from those who want to help him. He wants to learn and experience the world through his work and efforts. Speaking about the autonomy of independence Maria Montessori said:

*"We must clearly understand that when we give freedom and independence to the child we give freedom to a stimulated worker who cannot live except his work and activity."* [8]

## Discipline, Patience, and Good Manners

As we saw at the beginning of the chapter, the Montessori Method is based on the freedom of the child, a concept that was very difficult to accept in the 1950s when the discipline was very strict and consisted of stillness and silence. According to Maria, the discipline also had to consider the principle of freedom. A disciplined child is not silenced but one who is a master of himself and is capable of self-regulation. As the child learns to move in the environment, they prepare not for school but for life, becoming a *"correct individual by habit and practice."*[9] Discipline is thus not limited to the school environment but extends to society.

One way this happens is by maturing the quality of patience. In the Children's Homes, there were many learning materials to use, one different from the other; there was no duplication of the same object, and sometimes it happened that several children wanted to use the same one. At that time, the

---

[8] M. MONTESSORI, *The mind of the child,* Garzanti, Milan, 1952, 94.
[9] M. MONTESSORI, *Il Metodo della Pedagogia Scientifica applicato all'educazione infantile nelle Case dei Bambini*, Edizioni Opera Nazionale Montessori, Rome, 2000.

children learned patience: they did not fight over objects but waited their turn *"since this happens at every hour of the day, for years, the concept of respecting and waiting enters the life of every individual as an experience that matures over time."* [10]

When they used an object, they could do so for as long as they wished and thus enjoyed all the calm necessary for the creative genesis of the self that develops through continuous work. What the children learned from their experience was not merely teaching that served only in the school setting but allowed them to grow by developing virtues and qualities useful in society.

## Abolition of Rewards and Punishments

Montessori realized that giving rewards and chastising children only took away their dignity. Applying the above principles makes it possible to abolish rewards and chastisement and avoid making judgments by giving grades. Setting up the environment by providing suitable materials allows children to control their actions. This way, comparisons and evaluations are avoided, and self-esteem is cultivated from childhood.

## Contact with Nature

Another of Maria Montessori's fundamental goals was to get children to relate to Nature. Children who play outdoors not only grow in a much healthier way but also acquire information and lessons by experiencing the outdoor environment. Nature has a strong cognitive, emotional, and sensory impact and allows them to:

- Develop perceptions about their surroundings;
- Mature an extraordinary sensitivity to others and things by learning to care for them;

---

[10] M. MONTESSORI, *La mente del bambino,* Garzanti, Milan, 1952, 222.

- Acquire patience and healthy eating habits;
- Moving freely, running, climbing, keeping balanced;
- Have important sensory experiences.

Movement is also integral to learning in this context: children learn by moving and experiencing everything around them. By putting their hands in the soil, planting seeds, watching how plants grow or how leaves change color during the seasons, and caring for animals, children can acquire considerable skills, learn to classify plants, mature, and be responsible. All of this is also part of Montessori's "Cosmic Education," which believes that the love children cultivate for nature will enable them to become responsible and participating adults who can contribute to a general upliftment of society.

## How a Montessori School Works

In the Montessori school, children are not forced to listen to lessons in a completely passive way; on the contrary, their education takes place through a natural process using the experiences they have in the environment. In the Children's House, everyone is free to choose the activities to be performed and moves within the space without disturbing their classmates and waiting for their turn to be able to use the desired material; this approach allows them to learn both through imitation and direct experience. Classes are made up of children of different ages so that younger children can observe the different skills and behaviors of older children and learn by imitation. Of course, no grades or evaluations are given in this school, but only observation sheets describing the children's progress are filled out.

For the method to be successful, two elements are essential:

- A suitable space with the appropriate tools and materials to stimulate the child's learning;
- An educator who is present but at the same time merely observes the children without intervening in their activities.

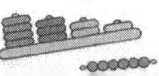

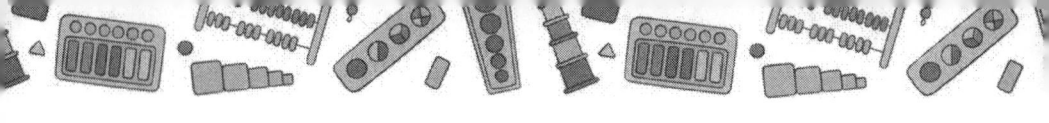

In Children's Homes, when they were shown something, they would exclaim, *"Me, I want to do it!"* and *"Help me do it myself."* Children love to learn and do; adults prevent them from doing things out of fear. Maria Montessori understood this and, in her remarks, stated:

> *"The adult must help the child, but for the child to act and carry out his or her work in the world."* [11]

The child's main need is expressed precisely in the phrase "Help me do it myself"; this statement reflects his innate drive to want to learn and learn independently, becoming increasingly capable, independent, and confident.

We mentioned earlier that the equipment is child-friendly and includes every suitable tool for daily activities, such as brooms, dustpans, sponges, cutlery, dishes, glasses, watering cans, hoes, rakes, etc. Children then learn every daily activity, such as washing the floors, setting the table, and tending the garden; this enables them to acquire many skills and competencies that are indispensable throughout their lives. In particular, the materials of objects are not unbreakable but are real; therefore, if children drop glass glasses or ceramic plates on the floor, they can learn through their mistakes to acquire greater control of their movements and care and attention to objects in the environment.

There are a few rules found within children's homes included in the Montessori Method, and they are:

1. Do not disturb or hit other children engaged in activities;
2. Use teaching objects and materials appropriately.

The word educate comes from the Latin word *"educere,"* translated as "to bring out." In keeping with this, the Montessori Method stipulates that educators' task is exclusively to observe children and help them bring out

---

[11] M. MONTESSORI, *Il segreto dell'infanzia*, Garzanti, Milan, 1950, 277.

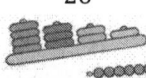

their interest and willingness to learn. Their task is to bring to light what is already present in the child. The latter is no longer seen as an empty vessel to be filled with theoretical teachings but as a unique being who already has within him all the knowledge and skills in potential and who, put in the right environment, can express and bring out the best version of himself in complete autonomy. [12]

## Abolition of Toys

During her experiments, Maria Montessori often placed beautiful toys among the educational materials; the consistent result was that no child picked them up. Toys are thus considered completely uneducational because children only request them when there is a lack of appropriate material, and when that is present, they are completely ignored and neglected.

## Role of the Teacher

The role of the teacher in Children's Homes is very different from that of a traditional teacher. She does not have a central role or a desk in the middle of the classroom. The teacher does not try to decant her knowledge into the child but learns from the child and directs all her energies in such a way as to help the child release and express her fullest potential during the activities and stages of learning. Teachers must demonstrate indispensable virtues such as calmness, patience, charity, and humility to succeed in this.

The teacher teaches the child not to need the adult and to do it himself; she does not give grades or judge. Her only job is to suggest age-appropriate material to the child and explain how it works. Each child is different from another, and what is suitable for one may not be suitable for another;

---

[12] M. MONTESSORI, *Educazione e pace*, Opera Nazionale Montessori, Rome, 2004.

therefore, the teacher must observe their children, their aptitudes and inclinations, and understand when they are ready for a particular activity.

## Scientific Evidence of the Method on Children

Experimenting with her method on poor children in Rome, Maria noticed that although she had done nothing to improve their physical condition, no one would recognize them anymore because their faces were colorful and their appearance was lively; those who at first seemed undernourished and anemic and in need of care were now healthy children as if they had received treatment. The main cause of the lack of vitality was psychic causes that affected the metabolism of the little ones. Enhancing the children's psyche improved their metabolism and all physical functions. This evidence aroused so much amazement in the people watching them that they came to speak of a real "miracle."

Everything the little ones learned in school, such as the importance of hygiene and personal care, they then passed on at home; as a result, parents learned to be cleaner and neater. Maria's children were slowly changing society: the adults were learning from the little ones.

Recent U.S. studies have shown that the specific Montessori Methodology is more effective than other methodologies in developing important neuropsychological functions implicated in school, work, and personal success as well as social skills. These studies examined emerging complex cognitive structures implicated in forming higher-order skills such as planning, organization, cognitive flexibility, and sustained attention. Dr. Angeline Lillard, professor of psychology at the University of Virginia and director of the Early Development Laboratory, and her colleagues sought to evaluate the constructive outcomes associated with the teaching and educational pathways inherent in Montessori Methodology. Specifically, these authors' study, which appeared in Science in 2006, compared tests of pupils from Montessori-method schools (at the end of Kindergarten and age

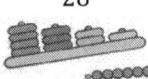

12) with those of pupils from a basic curriculum with other methodologies.[13] The comparison showed that children from preschools with a Montessori education had better outcomes on standardized tests in reading and mathematics, were more interactive in play, and were much more proficient in social-cognitive aspects and executive control. On the other hand, concerning children who had completed primary education, those from Montessori schools presented more creative forms of writing with more complex syntactic structures and chose more positive responses when faced with social issues, showing a greater sense of community. From the studies performed, it was clear that the Montessori Method provides greater learning, especially in executive functions and social-type problem-solving. It is very important because children from 0 to 3 years old with strong functional-executive skills accrue greater and stronger academic and social skills. "Executive functions" are critical for academic success and life.[14]

Thus, the Montessori Method still turns out to be one of the best educational methods for child development and growth.

---

[13] A.S. LILLARD - N. ELSE-QUEST, *The early years: evaluating Montessori Method*, Science, (2006), 313, 1893 at http://www.sciencemag.org/cgi/content/full/313/5795/1893.
[14] A.S. LILLARD, *Montessori: The science behind the genius*, New York, Oxford University Press, 2005.

## Chapter 3: The Development of the Child from 0 to 3 Years of Age

Dr. Montessori maintained that education begins from birth and that the early years of life are the most formative and important for the child's physical and mental development. Given how quickly the mind develops in the first five years, it is very important to apply an appropriate pedagogical method that can structure behavior patterns in the child that will determine their character in adulthood.

From birth, the child is open to external stimuli and, while having life experiences, goes through "psychic periods"; for example, he has a special sensitivity to objects, develops language, and learns to walk and move in space. By carefully observing the child, it is possible to identify the psychic period he is in so that he can be helped to master his environment.

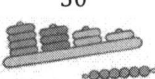

## The Sensitive Periods

According to Maria Montessori, children are guided in their development by well-marked times during which they accrue a special sensitivity to a particular type of learning; depending on the psychic period in which they are, the child's mind is better able to absorb stimuli from outside.

Children observe everything around them and can compare things through a "touchstone" that we do not possess; they compare external things with images in their minds. Toddlers also can remember and reproduce sounds of different languages, learn their words, and fix their accents.

In these learning brackets, children are more predisposed to achieve certain goals by engaging in activities that allow them to cultivate and grow a certain skill quite naturally and without the slightest effort. These types of sensitivities are transient so that later skills can be acquired. Failure to take advantage of the sensitivities of a specific time may jeopardize the child's psychic development, even in the long term. Therefore, we can define the psychic period as the **period of acquisition**: whatever the child learns during this age group can never again be obtained in a different age group or as an adult. [15]

There are 4 main sensory periods, and they vary in duration and intensity; these are:

- The sensory period of movement (0 to 4 years);
- The psychic period of love for the environment (0 to 6 years old);
- The psychic period of the order (0 to 4 years);
- The psychic period of language (0 to 6 years).

Let us analyze them more specifically.

---

[15] M. MONTESSORI, *The Method of Scientific Pedagogy applied to child education in Children's Homes*, Edizioni Opera Nazionale Montessori, Rome, 2000.

## Psychic Movement Period

In the first few years of life, the toddler soon learns to extend his arms, bring his fingers toward himself, pick up objects, crawl, and develop skills that make him independent. Visual-motor coordination gradually increases, and the toddler becomes increasingly confident until he has a firmer grip on objects and uses them properly; this confidence also prompts him to walk and even run.

During this stage, the toddler shows special interest in all activities that are important for his growth and personal development, which prepare him to achieve independence (such as dressing himself, brushing his teeth, washing his hands, dusting, removing leaves in the garden, etc.). When the toddler enters this psychic period, it may happen that he sometimes shows particular interest in a certain activity rather than another; this is completely normal since the toddler, when in the learning phase, focuses exclusively on one movement and repeats it many, many times until he masters it and can perform it to perfection, eliminating any margin for error.

## Sensitive Period of Love for the Environment

The sensory period of love for the environment occurs simultaneously with the other periods. As the toddler's senses develop, he begins to explore everything around him; at first, he will just look and listen, and then, as he acquires motor skills, his interest will be directed toward objects and the whole environment.

Thanks to the absorbing mind, the toddler learns a great deal by watching and moving in the space around him and does so very naturally and completely unconsciously. To facilitate this learning process and help the toddler absorb as much as possible and progress in its growth, the adult must remove all possible obstacles from the environment. Observing the children moving about inside the classroom, Maria Montessori realized that *"in the child's*

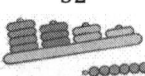

*environment everything must be measured as well as orderly, and that from the elimination of confusion and superfluity arise precisely interest and concentration."* [16]

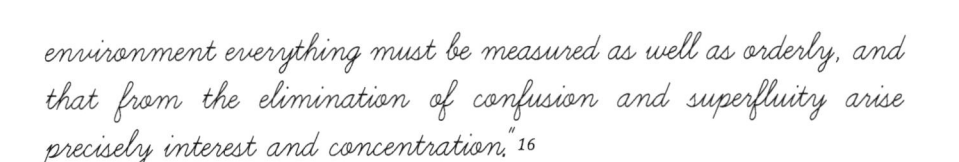

The little one loves to explore the environment, but the environment must reflect order and stimulate his interest to encourage maximum concentration while carrying out all activities. During this sensory period, the toddler learns that objects have a purpose, creating orderly structural patterns in his mind in which each object has a precise location according to its use. In the previous chapter, we mentioned that the Montessori Method requires that the environment be child-friendly so that the child has many stimuli and acquires many skills until they achieve independence; as we continue with the discussion, we will elaborate on this aspect and see how to create the ideal environment for the development of young children.

## Sensitive Period of the Order

Observing the children in her classrooms, it was clear to Maria Montessori that *"the child cannot live in disorder, for this causes him to suffer, and the suffering manifests itself in desperate crying and even in persistent agitation, which can take on the 'appearance of a real illness.'"* [17]

Maria illustrates the importance of this need through two examples: the first involves a little girl who, during a visit from a lady, begins to show signs of irritation and ill contentment and then bursts into excessive crying. When confronted with this scene, no one understands what happened, but at some point, the mother guesses that the toddler's discomfort was caused by the umbrella the lady had left on the table instead of placing it on the umbrella stand. Another example is when a toddler on a hike is in his mother's arms; at

---

[16] M. MONTESSORI, *Il segreto dell'infanzia*, Garzanti, Milan, 1950,162.
[17] M. MONTESSORI, *Il segreto dell'infanzia*, Garzanti, Milan, 1950, 68.

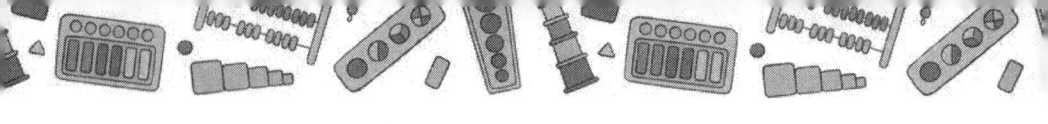

some point, the mother is hot and takes the jacket off her shoulders to hold it in her hands. For no obvious reason, the toddler bursts into a crying fit. Having witnessed the scene, Maria senses that the toddler's discomfort is caused by not seeing the mother's jacket in place and so suggests to the lady to put it back on her shoulders; having done so, the toddler immediately calms down.

During the psychic period of the order, the toddler needs to see things in the same place; above all, he needs to see them in the environment in which they are used (e.g., he needs to see the umbrella in the umbrella stand at the entrance, the vest worn, the toothbrush in the bathroom, the broom in the kitchen, etc. ). Seeing everything in its proper place gives the toddler a sense of gratification because his need for order is satisfied. In an orderly environment, the toddler can orient himself, concentrate, think, and metabolize his learning. An orderly environment allows him to build landmarks around him daily to evaluate the space around him and his emotions. Thus, the order is a fundamental characteristic of the environment.

When a toddler sees objects in the environment arranged disorderly, or differently than usual, he goes into crisis and tries to express his need for order through crying. Toddlers are very attentive to their surroundings and can notice details that we adults do not pay much attention to; therefore, we must try to look at the world through their eyes to understand their needs.

The Montessori Method respects the need for order by recreating orderly and functional environments so that the child feels comfortable, develops the ability to orient himself in space, and can perform all activities. During this period, the toddler learns about the placement of objects in the environment, how to remember where they are located, and the purpose for which they are used. This particular psychic period is very important for the child's growth and development as it enables him to learn to orient himself in the environment and master it.

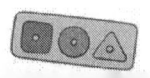

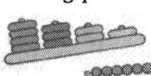

*Psychic Period of Language*

Language is the mode of communication we use to express ourselves and make ourselves understood by others. This method of communication begins as early as in the womb; in fact, the fetus can perceive sounds. After birth, the baby begins distinguishing sounds from noises and gradually can recognize voices. The infant's main mode of communication is crying, but he can also react to sound stimuli and recognize their exact origin; during this stage, he can learn and recognize words in all world languages, but his focus is on the language used to communicate in his environment.

The sensory period of language is thus an unconscious learning phase that enables the toddler to absorb everything he hears and reproduce the sound spontaneously and without the slightest effort. He gradually succeeds in developing his ability to hear and reproduce sounds; he first begins with a phase of lallation in which he reproduces vocalizations and syllables, gradually progressing to the pronunciation of words, sentences composed of subject and verb, and finally sentences with a rich vocabulary and grammatically correct articulations. By the end of this period, the toddler will be fully able to communicate even with strangers, tell stories, and express his curiosity through questions.

## Stages of Development

The psychic period is a complex process of growth. Analyzing the stages of the toddler's metamorphosis that occur in the first 3 years of life will enable us to understand better the learning mechanisms, psychomotor development, and growth. This developmental process can be divided into 8 stages, each of which is characterized by a targeted educational project to enhance the toddler's abilities. We analyze each stage by highlighting what happens in the motor, sensory, language, and cognitive-relational areas.

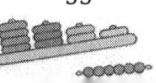

## Before Birth

**Motor Scope:** from the 20th week, the fetus becomes more active, and the mother begins to sense its movements.

**Sensory and Speech Scope:** the ears develop, which allows the baby to begin to perceive noises. In the 25th week, the fetus can recognize familiar sounds, particularly the mother's voice.

**Cognitive and Relational Scope:** by recognizing voices, the baby can respond through movement.

## Birth

**Motor Scope:** the newborn's reactions are dictated by his instincts. The head begins to be supported by neck strength, and gradually the baby learns to keep the body and hands extended.

**Sensory and Language Scope:** sight, smell, and hearing are not fully developed but still allow the baby to recognize the mother and all words in any language.

**Cognitive and Relational Scope:** the baby communicates mainly through crying.

## 0 to 3 Months

**Motor Scope:** babies increase their ability to control their head, which they can hold up even on their stomach, and hands, which they can bring to their mouth and with which he begins to grasp objects.

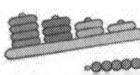

**Sensory and Language Domain:** they begin to develop the ability to follow gaze and focus on a face, to produce sounds with crying and shrieking, and to react in response to sound stimuli.

**Cognitive and Relational Domain:** they develop adaptive skills toward their surroundings, distinguish what they like from what they don't, and share their affective states.

## 3 TO 4 MONTHS

**Motor Scope:** babies lift their heads better, grasp objects, shake them, and bring them to their mouth.

**Sensory and Language Scope:** they can follow moving objects and recognize familiar faces at a distance; they can locate sounds and recognize their mother's voice.

**Cognitive and Relational Scope:** they respond with vowels when those around them speak and smile.

## 5 TO 6 MONTHS

**Motor Scope:** through visual development, babies begin to grasp and wave objects with their hands and develop facial-motor coordination.

**Sensory and Language Scope:** babies begin to turn toward the speaker visually, follow their movements and those of their tools, and recognize familiar objects and people at a distance even better; they begin to produce vocalizations, repeat syllables composed of the same consonant, and react more actively to sounds around him by distinguishing the direction from which the sound is coming and sometimes trying to imitate it.

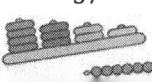

**Cognitive and Relational Scope:** the baby develops expressive skills through both face and body movements and smiles spontaneously at the adult. It is a period during which he plays a lot.

## 7 TO 10 MONTHS

**Motor Scope:** the baby can sit with or without support and controls the head and trunk well. Motor development is very evident at this stage as he can sit, roll, crawl, crawl, and sometimes even stand while trying to maintain balance; he can also bend at the knees and grasp objects with both hands.

**Sensory and Language Scope:** this stage is very important for language development. The baby responds to sounds, learns to pronounce syllables with different consonants, has a richer lallation, and develops a broader vocabulary. Visually, he has full-color vision and can follow moving objects with his eyes.

**Cognitive and Relational Scope:** recognizes his favorite games; develops the ability to organize through his routine and plays with his parents; begins to look at himself in the mirror; responds to the emotions of those around him and reacts in different ways when faced with strangers. He understands individual words and indicates what he wants with his finger. He also strengthens his memory skills.

## 11 TO 13 MONTHS

**Motor Scope:** the baby can sit up, support his weight on his legs, grasp objects in a coordinated way, locate partially visible objects, and strives to reach those that are not within his reach; he is very curious to discover everything in the environment and learns to walk by leaning on furniture.

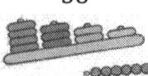

**Sensory and Language Domain:** distance vision is fully developed, and his ability to follow moving objects and people increases; at this stage, he learns to pronounce his first words related to the environment (mostly with nasal-sounding consonants such as mommy and daddy).

**Cognitive and Relational Domain:** he tries to communicate with the adult and can understand short sentences and simple orders. During this stage, he can express his feelings and emotions through his voice and begins to manifest early character traits such as shyness or nervousness.

## 14 TO 18 MONTHS

**Motor Scope:** this is one of the most important stages because it determines the toddler's independence as he learns the purpose of each object and its use, can use a spoon by himself, plays with clothes, can take objects out of a container and put them back in place; he also walks, runs and drags objects with him.

**Sensory and Language Scope:** his vocabulary gradually expands up to 50 words. This stage determines the beginning of the vocabulary explosion: the toddler can understand that each word corresponds to an object and can express himself using language.

**Cognitive and Relational Scope:** he can think and imagine. He tries to gain more independence by eating and dressing; he is very happy to be together with his peers and shows his affection in an obvious way.

## 19 MONTHS TO 2 YEARS

**Motor Scope:** the toddler is fully autonomous; he climbs and descends stairs holding onto support but without help; motor coordination is more evident as he can copy simple signs and recognize shapes. He can use pincer grasping to put objects in order inside a container.

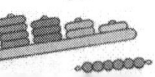

**Sensory and Language Scope:** can pronounce both words and simple sentences, responds when asked questions, understand what others say, and carries out remote commands.

**Cognitive and Relational Scope:** during this phase, there is extraordinary cognitive development; the toddler can use objects according to their purpose, pays attention to speech and response, easily finds objects, and tries to imitate others. They love to spend time with peers and adults, using their vivid imaginations to simulate everyday activities together. They show affection, shyness, and concern and are intimidated by the distance of their parents. Despite this, they always seek to make discoveries cautiously under their supervision.

## 2 to 3 years old

**Motor Scope:** walks without stumbling, runs, can climb and descend stairs by alternating feet, and can jump, pedal, and kick; pulls toys toward him and carries large toys; can draw and copy circles correctly using a pencil and cut using scissors; completes small puzzles and builds towers.

**Sensory and Language Scope:** can recognize colors and body parts and combine shapes. He speaks intelligibly even to strangers, masters grammar rules, answers questions, and can tell small stories. His ability to pronounce sounds improves dramatically, his vocabulary becomes richer and more varied, and he can express himself using more than 500 words; he acquires morphosyntactic skills that enable him to produce simple sentences composed of subject and verb.

**Cognitive and Relational Scope:** during this stage, the toddler shows emotions such as shame, pride, and possessiveness and socializes with adults and toddlers his age by carrying out activities together while respecting rules. He begins to understand gender differences, shows greater independence, and is excited by the company of peers.

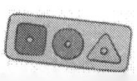

# Chapter 4: The Needs of the 0 to 3-Year-Old Child

Many living beings have needs they seek to satisfy, which is also true for toddlers. These needs concern not only the physical sphere, such as the need to eat or sleep but also the emotional sphere and must be met for the little one to have healthy growth and development. But what exactly are the needs of a toddler from 0 to 3 years old?

His needs are indeed many. Some of them we have already mentioned in talking about the psychic periods. We have seen that a toddler needs to be surrounded to build fixed landmarks in his mind; he needs to move, to discover the environment by himself through the five senses, and he needs to do. All other needs of the toddler are always related to the sensory periods and are:

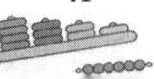

- Need for direct contact with the mother;
- Need to feel protected and safe;
- Need to develop relationships;
- Need to find stable reference points;
- Need its biological rhythms to be respected;
- Need for self-awareness as an individual;
- Need for freedom and independence;
- Need for a tailored space;
- Need for concentration;
- Need to use hands;
- Need to experience nature;
- Need for silence.

We will now go into more detail about these additional needs of the toddler so that we have a clear idea of how to succeed in meeting them.

## The Need for Direct Contact with the Mother

Direct contact with the mother is one of the infant's main needs. At birth, he depends on her, learning to recognize her smell and voice and trying to communicate with her through crying and body movements. The mother-child relationship has always been studied with special attention because it is precisely this primordial bond that will influence all of the infant's future relationships and rapport, although he will relate to many figures who will be important throughout his life (father, grandparents, siblings, etc.), the mother-child attachment creates a very deep imprint in the way the child will see himself with others and will expect to be accepted, loved and understood in his uniqueness.

Mother-child attachment can be of two types:

- **Safe**: it allows for the maturation of adults with good dialogue skills listening skills, who knows their needs and can talk about them;

- **Insecure**: involves a whole range of fears and behaviors resulting from the fear of abandonment. Children raised with insecure attachments will grow into adults with difficulty relating, insecurity about themselves, and constant fear of abandonment.

Therefore, the mother needs to give proper attention to the baby from birth and take care to meet all needs to raise the infant in a safe environment conducive to healthy development.

## The Need to Feel Protected and Safe

An infant needs to feel protected and live in a safe environment. It will give him serenity and peace, and he will grow up without experiencing feelings of fear and insecurity that would be devastating at this delicate stage of personality growth and development. Toddlers who feel protected grow up calm, confident, and self-assured. But how can parents make a toddler feel safe and secure?

One way they can do this is by expressing appreciation toward him. A toddler feels protected when his parents meet his basic needs and can perceive and understand all his emotions by giving a reliable response on time. When the little one perceives his parents' love, he feels protected and understood and trusts that he will be comforted when he is sad; the infant has the confidence that nothing bad will happen to him when angry and that someone will protect him when he is afraid. All this gives him a deep inner calm and strengthens his self-esteem.

## The Need to Develop Relationships

From birth, the baby seeks to communicate and establish a strong bond with the caregiver, that is, the caregiver figure, primarily the mother. As the baby bonds with his mother and creates an increasingly strong bond with her, he learns to self-regulate his behaviors through the feedback reactions he receives. Contact with the caregiver is also fostered by his physiological needs, such as eating and sleeping; these time structures allow the baby to develop his perceptions. Over time he also learns to do so with other parental figures to the point of relating to people outside the family unit.

## The Need to Find Stable Landmarks

To grow up well, a baby also needs stable points of reference. The most important reference point is the one given by his parents. Thanks to their example, he learns and distinguishes right from wrong; moreover, the certainty that his parents love him no matter what allows him to grow up with self-esteem, self-confidence, and security.

In addition to the parental figures who constitute the greatest point of reference, the baby also needs to identify other firm points of reference; some of these can be found in the environment. Speaking of order, we have already mentioned how important it is for babies that their surroundings be orderly and organized; order allows the baby to identify stable reference points that enable him to create his optimistic and serene view of reality and structure an inner order that will influence the formation of his character.

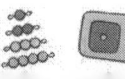

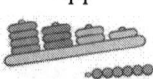

Order is not only important on a superficial level but also in terms of rules and routines; for example, always being dressed and undressed according to a certain order, having scanned schedules for meals, waking up and falling asleep, always wanting the same person to help them, etc. Although these details may seem insignificant to adults, they are very important to the little one; the moment the need to find points of reference is not respected, unpleasant consequences can occur in the baby's psyche, who will try to express his suffering through screaming, anger and uncontrollable crying. When faced with these situations, the adult must remain calm and understand the unmet need that produces suffering in the baby and triggers those seemingly exaggerated reactions. It must always be remembered that babies pay attention to details that sometimes go unnoticed by us and that there is always a rational inner explanation behind apparently illogical behavior.

Satisfying the baby's need to find stable reference points will enable him to orient himself spatially, relationally, and temporally and develop the necessary internal security that will enable him to act in the world.

## The Need for His Biological Rhythms to be Respected

Toddlers need to live in a slow time; it is necessary to respect their biological rhythms, that is, to allow them to eat when they are hungry and sleep when they are. In this regard, Maria wrote:

> *"The child should have the right to sleep when he is sleepy and to wake up when he is done sleeping and get up when he wants to. So we recommend, and already many families are implementing it, the 'abolition of the classic toddler bed and its replacement with a very low bed, almost skimming the ground where the child can sit and get up at will."* [18]

The Montessori Method is based on observing toddlers to meet their needs and fulfill their requirements. Respecting the toddler's biological rhythms will allow, as we saw in the previous paragraph, to create stable points of reference in the toddler's mind and make the child gradually more and more independent. To meet this need, Montessori has devised alternative beds to the classic ones: mats placed on the floor that allow the toddler to get up and go to sleep on his own without anyone's help.

---

[18] M. MONTESSORI, *Il segreto dell'infanzia*, Garzanti, Milan, 1950,99.

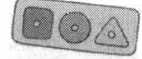

Another occasion when the toddler's time can be respected is when the toddler focuses on discovery and practice. On these occasions, the little one practices by repeating the same movement and actions several times until he performs them to perfection. He does not get tired from working; on the contrary, he grows because the work allows him to develop and refine his skills. When he is focused and immersed in these activities, do not distract him for futile reasons because these moments are crucial for building mental landmarks. Respecting his biological rhythms will help him focus and be responsible and autonomous.

## *The Need for Self-Awareness as an Individual*

Another very important need for the toddler is to become aware of himself as an individual and to have experiences that bring out his personality. The Montessori Method's main purpose is to help each toddler express their fullest potential and be the best version of themselves. Related to this need is the Montessori principle of freedom. For a toddler to become self-aware, they must be free to move, do, and discover; only then can they learn to self-regulate and develop qualities such as patience and prudence. Leaving toddlers free does not mean that there are no healthy rules or they are exposed to danger without protection. It means helping them to develop a deep sense of responsibility from an early age.

Speaking of the "dangerous" activities carried out in the Children's Home, Maria Montessori said:

> *"The facts that are real and common to our children refer to a "prudence" that enables them to avoid dangers and therefore to live among them. Such as being able to handle knives at the dinner table, and also in the kitchen, handle matches, or light objects,*

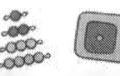

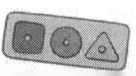

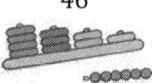

*light a fire, remain unguarded in pools of water or cross a street in the city. In short, our children can control acts and together recklessness, composing a serene and superior form of life. Normalization, therefore, does not correspond to throwing oneself into dangers, but to developing prudence that allows one to act amidst dangers, knowing and mastering them."* [19]

Leaving the child free to act, to make mistakes, and try again without saying, "you're doing it wrong," "watch out, you'll get hurt," or "no! this is not done," will allow the child to grow up with great confidence in their abilities, to pick themselves up despite mistakes, and to try again until they achieve their goals. Very often, extremely caring parents stifle the child by not letting them have experienced, but children have a need to do; satisfying this need by allowing them the freedom to experiment and learn from their mistakes will allow them to develop autonomy and achieve increased degrees of independence.

## The Need for Freedom and Independence

We have already seen that freedom is one of the core principles underlying the Montessori Method and its main goal. Freedom is very important for the child to acquire and develop skills that will lead them to achieve independence by performing tasks and working "on his own." From the moment the child begins to take his first steps and refine coordination skills, he tries to assert his need for freedom and independence. Gradually he tries to immerse himself in activities that excite him to the point of wanting to make himself useful by performing small tasks within his reach. The child has a great desire to know what works for him; for him is a source of learning; he

---

[19] M. MONTESSORI, *Il segreto dell'infanzia*, Garzanti, Milan, 1950, 241.

does not get tired by working, but it increases his energy and improves his development. Many times, the adult, believing that he is doing the child's good, tries to dispense him from activities that might be tiring or time-consuming and gives him rest, but in doing so, he goes against his needs. Precisely concerning this issue, Maria Montessori said:

> *"Who does not understand that teaching a child to eat, to wash, to dress, is far more time-consuming, difficult, and patient work than feeding, washing, and dressing him. All of it is useless to help, it impedes the development of natural forces."* [20]

Although it may be more comfortable to carry the baby in your arms or a baby carriage or dress him, don't do it! Let him do it on his own. It means that it will take him longer to walk a stretch of road on his own, dress, tie his shoes, and wash, but doing all these activities on his own will allow him to gain confidence and reach an increasing degree of freedom and independence. The adult just needs to be very patient and let the child meet these needs.

## The Need for a Tailor-made Space

The child needs to be in a space tailored to him at all stages of his growth. Since his "measurements" change quickly, to meet this need, it is necessary to progressively adjust some spaces in the house according to his needs. Let's see how this can be done.

From the third month onward, the baby develops vision and facial-motor coordination. Sensory enhancement enables him to look around and act in the environment, so he needs a tailored space that allows him not only to look around but also to move.

---

[20] M. MONTESSORI, *Educare alla libertà*, Laterza, Bari, 1950, 49-50.

Next, he moves from his mother's arms to the floor. During this stage, it would be wise to use a mat of at least one square meter on which he can begin his journey of exploration on his stomach.

At 8 months old, he has a few more needs: he needs not only a soft, well-defined space but also a horizontal mirror, rattles, and a treasure basket. As soon as he can move independently, he will wish to have a larger surface area at his disposal. It is necessary to organize his room and make small changes in the common areas to meet his needs.

By the time he is 2 years old, he will be autonomous in walking and will try to reach out and take hold of anything that arouses his curiosity. It would therefore be advisable to remove all unbreakable and dangerous objects from his reach, not only because he might break them and hurt himself but also because not being able to pick them up might generate his feelings of frustration and crisis. In the second part of this book, we will look more specifically at how to furnish certain home spaces to satisfy the child's needs.

## *The Need for Concentration*

Concentration is the ability to fix attention on a specific item or activity persistently. This ability is not acquired in adulthood but manifests in infants as early as a few weeks. They focus very much on stimuli from outside, such as the movements of objects suspended over the crib, voices, and everything around them. As they grow, their concentration ability increases, and they can perform real activities to achieve visual-motor coordination. When a toddler is deeply focused on his work, nothing and no one can distract him from his activity, not even background noises.

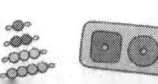

Concentration thus implies an absolute focus on the goal to be achieved; from this comes strong positivity and gratification for one's work. The greater the concentration, the greater the chance that all external distractions will be completely ignored (even if they are physiological needs). The engine of concentration interests. As we have seen, the Montessori Method requires that toddlers be allowed to choose the work material; this means that when the toddlers choose, it is because they have a strong interest in that particular activity. The intensity of concentration varies according to different age groups; for example, at 6 months, the toddler spends a lot of time transferring objects from one hand to the other, while at 15, he tries to carry heavy objects by exercising simultaneous coordination of the upper and lower limbs.

The need for concentration results in the repetition of the action until perfection is achieved. The toddler repeatedly completes the exercise until he satisfies his inner need. Concentration enables him to develop other qualities such as patience, persistence, and self-discipline, which prompted him to practice and correct his mistakes until he completely controls his actions.

But how can we help toddlers on this path? It is necessary to pay attention to several factors:

- **Limit stimuli**: toddlers do not need a lot of stimuli but need them to be few and of quality. Too many stimuli prevent them from concentrating because their attention moves quickly from one stimulus to another without really focusing on anything.

- **Isolate qualities:** we said that the material to be offered to the toddler should be few and well selected. It would be best to avoid objects that have too many materials and colors; they should have few clear and appreciable qualities. If, for example, your goal is to get the toddler to focus on smells, you can offer him smell bags of the same material and size but containing different types of spices. It will make it easier for the toddler to focus all his attention on the sense of smell.

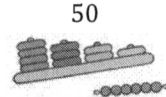

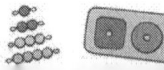

- **Do not interrupt them unnecessarily:** you must respect every activity toddlers do without interrupting them. However, it may seem like a trivial activity, such as opening and closing a drawer, but to engage in that action, the toddler makes a considerable mental and muscular effort. It is, therefore, necessary to remain silent. Even receiving praise can be distracting and end an experience of inner enrichment and psychic development. Concentration allows the toddler to develop his mind and build his personality. Therefore, it is very important to allow toddlers time to finish the activity in which they are immersed.

## The Need to Use Hands

In her book *"Il segreto dell'infanzia"* (The Secret of Childhood), Maria Montessori defined the hand as:

> *"that fine organ, complicated in its structure, which enables intelligence not only to manifest itself but to enter into special relationships with the environment."* [21]

Thus, hands are the toddler's first tool to achieve his goals, explore and increase his knowledge by experiencing his surroundings. From her studies, Maria Montessori also learned that:

> *"if due to special conditions of the environment, the child cannot make use of his hand, his character remains at a very low level, he remains incapable of obedience, initiative, lazy and sad; while the child who has been able to work with his hands reveals marked development and strength of character."* [22]

The use of hands has a strong impact on the toddler's mind as he first thinks and then acts using his little hands. Repetition of movements allows the

---
[21] M. MONTESSORI, *Il segreto dell'infanzia*, Garzanti, Milan, 1950,108.
[22] M. MONTESSORI, *La mente del bambino*, Garzanti, Milan, 1952, 152.

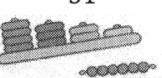

toddler to develop coordination, and the more he practices performing a given movement, the better his execution and coordination will be. At first, he will just study objects in his hands, then he will perform more precise movements such as interlocking, and as he grows, he will be able to perform activities of daily living such as washing dishes, sweeping the floor, sewing, etc. All these activities develop the toddler's mind tremendously and build his personality and character. In this regard, Maria points out that:

> *"All these exercises that promote movement coordination are done to achieve a defined purpose, considered by the mind. In these exercises, children not only move their muscles but also put their mind in order and enrich it."* [23]

A toddler engaged in activities and completely immersed in them demonstrates, as Montessori said, not only great "strength of character" but also the ability to create "order" in his mind. The most recent neuropsychiatric studies have shown that the toddler's mind processes abstract principles necessary for cognitive development through observation and movement. In that way, the toddler learns and stores a large number of procedural information packets and lays a solid foundation for transforming the movements he has made his own into abstract concepts.

One way to help your toddler meet this need is to provide appropriate materials for different stages of learning and allow him to perform easy household tasks.

---

[23] M. MONTESSORI, *La scoperta del bambino*, Garzanti, Milan, 1970,332.

## The Need to Experience Nature

Another very important need for the toddler is to experience nature. Children's Homes are very sensitive about this issue; to meet this need, they have gardens, plants, vegetable gardens, and even animals such as birds or fish. If you have the opportunity, you can adopt a pet so your toddler can learn to care for it.

The increasingly technological age in which we live is driving children and adults away from nature. Very often, children are left to the "care" of TV and tablets without a time limit and rarely have experiences in nature. Children need to discover nature. If you live in places surrounded by nature, such as the countryside, the sea, and the mountains, take every opportunity possible to put your toddler in touch with the surrounding nature. If, on the other hand, you live in the city, you can take advantage of the green spaces available to you, such as parks and gardens. You can play with leaves, let them discover the different animals there, play with puddles, pick flowers, etc. In the second part of this guide, we have reserved a space dedicated to simple and fun outdoor activities that you can do together with your little one to encourage contact with nature and allow him to develop a strong sensitivity, curiosity, and respect for his surroundings and great civic sense.

## The Need for Silence

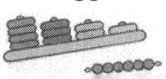

During her studies made of observations and understanding of child behavior, Maria Montessori understood that silence is one of the child's fundamental needs; that is why one of the principles of her Method is precisely the conquest of silence and the satisfaction of this need. We have already mentioned the importance of silence and the fact that it is a great achievement for the child. In traditional schools, silence is imposed as a punishment; Maria Montessori, on the other hand, saw silence as a precious element to be sought after. Only in silence is it possible to have maximum concentration and to dwell on sounds and details that noise and confusion prevent one from noticing. The achievement of silence promotes harmony.

Since children learn most by doing and playing, Maria Montessori invented the silence game to make them understand the beauty and great power of silence. During the game, children had to be quiet as long as possible and listen to the sounds made by birds, wind, and rain. During this game, everyone was very enthusiastic. Silence gave children an additional opportunity to learn, live more deeply, discover, concentrate, and create order in their minds.

# Chapter 5: The Role of the Parent

In the previous chapters, we have seen that the Montessori Method is based on the child's freedom, self-education, independence, and self-discipline. It would almost seem that the parent figure has little relevance to growth and learning. What then is the role of the parent?

Although the child learns about the world independently, the parent figure is very important: his task is to be a guiding spirit. The adult must help the toddler to do their work in the world; the child must guide the toddler on their growth path by identifying their needs in the different age groups and offering them appropriate activities for gradual and complete development. To form toddlers who are free, happy, and able to make their own choices independently and autonomously, the parent must consider several factors. Let's look at some of them.

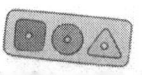

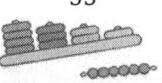

## Treat Your Child with Respect

Treat your child with the same respect you would show to an adult you value. Don't give him orders but communicate with him calmly and patiently by putting yourself on the same level as him; don't look down on him but lower yourself and look him straight in the eye when you speak; don't talk about him, or even worse, badmouth him in front of other people. Try to build a relationship based on mutual respect without forcing him to show affection and hug you if he does not want to; rather, take advantage of the occasions when he wants to. This way, you will treat your child respectfully, just as if he were a small adult.

## Meet His Needs

In the previous chapter, we saw the needs of a toddler from zero to three years old; your job as a parent is to meet them. Toddlers don't have the conception of time that adults have, nor can they understand it. Therefore, do not set times for him to eat or sleep but strive to respect **his** biological **rhythms**. Take time to re-read the toddler's needs and always ask what you can improve to facilitate his growth and development.

## Follow His Interests

To follow your toddler's interests, you must practice every day observing him silently and leaving him free to express himself; in a manner you will be able to understand what he is interested in. To develop this observational skill, creating an environment around your little one piques his interest is important. As we have seen, respecting his freedom does not mean leaving him to his own devices and in an environment full of dangers. Your job is to watch over him while leaving him the opportunity to express his creativity and to correct him in the face of potentially dangerous situations.

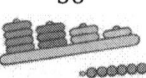

## Communicate and Involve Him

From an early age, even though the toddler may seem very young, you can understand, communicate with him, talk to him, and involve him in activities. Even if he cannot respond or express himself, he understands you and develops his understanding skills daily. Therefore, consider him as a thinking individual from the very beginning.

## Use Positive Discipline

When you relate to your toddler, you must have a great deal of patience. It also implies **avoiding verbal or physical punishment**, shouting at and threatening him, and affixing negative nicknames, such as "naughty." Encourage him and use positive discipline without punishing him but explaining to him the reasons why he should not do a certain thing, for example, by explaining to him the consequences of a dangerous situation; this does not mean that you have to point out all situations to him, but you have to help him understand what is good and what is bad so that he can metabolize an explanation of it. So, if he wants to do something but cannot do it because it is dangerous, don't just say, "stand still!" or "don't do that!" or "you will get hurt!" but **very calmly and patiently** explain to him what might happen and what he might be up against.

When he throws tantrums, try to understand what the real reason is that causes his discomfort or lack of need that leads him to cry and scream. What for us are incomprehensible overreactions for toddlers is a way of expressing an inner discomfort. Trying to understand them fully will help them develop self-confidence and positivity even when dealing with others. After all, toddlers are sponges, so how parents relate to them will be reflected in how the little ones relate to others.

But is it possible to avoid a toddler's outbursts? Sometimes yes; let's see how:

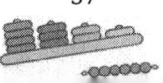

- Avoid places that may tire or excite him;
- Tell them in advance what you will do or where you will go, and then keep your promise;
- Set limits and explain in advance to the toddler what you will or will not do or what you will buy and what you are not willing to buy, and then do not give in (your "yes" must be "yes" and "no" "no")
- Do things slowly and quietly;
- Create enjoyable routines with your toddler such as doing activities together or reading a book at the same time.

Sometimes, however, it is not enough to do everything to prevent your toddler's outbursts because as he grows up, he will always try to challenge these limits. What to do then when your toddler has an outburst?

- Remain calm and do not resort to force threats or violence;
- Calmly take him aside and talk to him calmly, always trying to understand the reason for his anger;
- Try to console him while always maintaining a positive, calm, and understanding attitude;
- Isolating him will help him reflect and calm down;
- Finally, ask him if he is better and show him that you are not angry with him through cuddling.

## Allow Them to Try New Experiences

Do not prevent your toddler from trying new experiences just because you think they are beyond THEIR reach. Toddlers need to discover their limits, and they can only do this by gaining experience. Even if some activities are inappropriate for their age, let them try them; this way, they will develop the ability to self-regulate and distinguish what they can and cannot yet do. Have confidence in them and allow them to do different kinds of activities, including domestic ones. When you allow them to participate in daily tasks, they can practice, acquire new skills and feel gratification for their work.

## Do Not Interrupt the Flow of Concentration

In the previous chapter, we discussed the toddler's need for concentration. When you see your toddler immersed in a certain activity, let him work quietly and do not interrupt his concentration; at that moment, the toddler's mind is working actively to build mental patterns. Interrupting this process can cause damage to learning. Do not interrupt him unnecessarily with your words but allow him time to finish his activity in silence; this will promote his concentration.

## Propose Choices for Them

Allow your toddler to choose what he prefers. For example, if he is learning to dress, allow him to choose what to wear by providing him with options, or if he is to snack, give him options from which to choose. When you allow your toddler to make free choices without imposing things on him, you give him a chance to develop the faculty to make decisions, to reason, and to understand what his needs are; you will help him to become a confident adult, capable of reasoning and making decisions.

## Limit the Number of Games Available to Him

Observing toddlers in children's homes, Maria noticed that although there were many toys to choose from, toddlers ignored them completely to engage in productive activities. It makes us realize that it is not necessary to overwhelm toddlers with toys but to provide them with materials that will make them curious and enable them to "do" to develop skills and abilities. Toddlers choose toys only out of boredom when not presented with an activity that gratifies them.

When buying toys for your toddler, ask yourself: what purpose do they serve? Do they help my toddler make decisions? Do they encourage him to explore and use his hands?

Do not provide too much material because it may distract the toddler and prevent him from concentrating; provide little material at a time, and as he grows, also teach him to tidy up as soon as he finishes the activity he wants.

## Encourage but Do Not Reward

One of the principles of the Montessori Method is the abolition of chastisement rewards from children's classes. Parents can also abide by this principle by not rewarding their children with expressions such as "how clever you are!" or "you are so good!" Rejoice in your child's successes, but only when he makes real progress; do not congratulate him on anything he does. If, for example, he set the table himself, instead of saying what a good boy you can say I like the way you set the table. Such an approach is much more rewarding than being praised for anything. Remember to dignify him and show him respect just as you would an adult.

## Always Tell Them the Truth

Trust is the foundation of all relationships. Always strive to cultivate it with your toddler as well. Do not lie to him or make promises you cannot keep. Explain to him the reasons for your decisions in a simple way; if, for example, you have to entrust him to someone, tell him why you have to go away and also when you will return; do not leave him without notifying him otherwise you might cause unnecessary separation anxiety in him, and he might have overreactions in case it happens again.

## Turn off the TV

Parents often leave their toddlers in the care of "babysitting television." Numerous studies have shown that leaving one's children for hours on end in front of the TV inhibits their learning faculties. The rapid succession of images and sounds prevents children from concentrating and can cause speech and learning disorders. So, turn off the TV and engage your child in activities that allow him to experiment through the 5 senses and develop language, motor, and cognitive skills. Get his mind working and allow him to do and experiment. In the second part of this guide, you will find many useful hints of hands-on activities you can propose and perform with him.

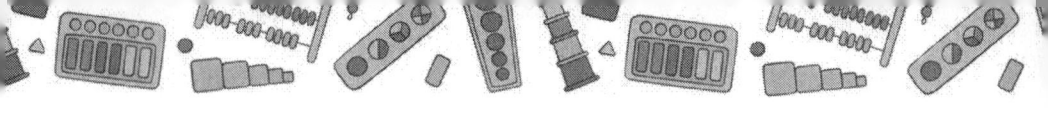

# Part II: Montessori Activities

## Chapter 6: Organizing the Home According to the Montessori Method

The Montessori Method is not a method that is applied exclusively in the school environment but can also be applied in the home. Organizing spaces according to the Montessori Method makes it possible to:

- Encourage the little one to be self-reliant and independent;
- Make him participate and be active in the management of household chores;
- Provide him with personalized spaces where he can relax, create and grow;
- Developing his concentration;
- Develop his sense of responsibility for his belongings.

In this chapter, we will look at how we can organize rooms to meet the needs of toddlers and develop their skills, autonomy, creativity, and decision-making abilities. The environment in which the toddler will spend most of his time is the nursery, and it is on the organization of this environment that we will focus most; next, we will look at other rooms in the house and see how they can be organized in a way that, in general, stimulates toddlers' interest and facilitates their activities.

# 5 Tips for Organizing Your Home in the Montessori Style

## Child-friendly

Just as Children's Homes are characterized by child-friendly furnishings, try to arrange the furniture so that the toddler has custom-made corners in the house where there are low tables, small chairs, bookshelves, and items that he can carry on his own without asking for help.

## From His Point of View

When organizing the house, try to put yourself in his shoes by lowering yourself to his height and looking through his eyes. This way, you will be able to notice dangers or problems in the environment to remedy.

## Order

We have seen that order is a basic need of the toddler. Organize the house and spaces used by the little one so that each material has a dedicated place according to its purpose and use. For example, create a corner for reading, one for sleeping, etc. In this way, he can train his sense of internal order. We will elaborate more on this by analyzing the characteristics of each room in the house.

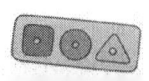

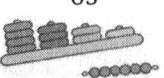

## Less Is More

Toddlers prefer simple but well-organized, clean, and neat spaces. These characteristics enable them to develop strong concentration and create order in their minds and thoughts. Offer them a few activities at a time so that they can focus their attention on them without unnecessary distractions. Provide additional activities only when the toddler has mastered the ones already present and is bored with them.

## Nature at Home

The Montessori Method requires toddlers to develop a strong connection with nature by observing and meditating on it. One way you can meet this need of hers at home is by decorating some spaces in the house with plants. When your toddler observes them, they dwell on how they grow, change and develop; they learn that they need water to grow and how to care for them, maturing a strong sense of ethics.

## The Nursery

A toddler's bedroom should be considered a multifunctional space because this is where he will carry out different activities such as sleeping, playing, reading, and lounging; therefore, the bedroom contains the whole world of the toddler. It should be a warm, relaxing environment that inspires tranquility. To this end, care should be taken when choosing wall colors, preferring neutral and light solid colors; if you choose an ivory color, this will reflect a warm light throughout the room. Since the purpose is to stimulate the child's observation and imagination, you can apply wallpaper on the walls with designs representing mountains, a landscape, a forest, the sea, or constellations and space. You can have it done by a decorator or, if the designs are as simple as mountains, you can do it yourself with the help of paper tape.

Furnishing a Montessori-style bedroom, therefore, means applying the educational principles of her Method through furniture of a certain type in such a way that the toddler feels free and independent. The nursery should be a space proportioned to the toddler's size; all the furniture present, including light switches, should be able to be used by the toddler and operated without adult help. Choose a few items to keep and ensure the room is always tidy; items should be of good quality, at the toddler's height, and attract his attention. All these arrangements will stimulate him to become more and more independent: since everything is tailor-made and within his reach, he will be able to choose independently whether to rest, sleep, read, or play, being physically and also psychologically able to carry out these activities on his own.

Let us look specifically at the elements found within a Montessori bedroom set.

## The Bed

In the first few days, the newborn needs an environment that reminds him of his mother's womb. Therefore, it is important to keep him wrapped to recreate the same feeling inside his mother's belly and protect him. You can use the "topponcino": a mat placed on the bottom of the basket and the bed, ideal for cradling the newborn and carrying him.

As the toddler grows, you can move him to a bed; this should be low and should not exceed 25 cm, including the mattress so that the toddler will not hurt himself trying to climb up or down independently. You should also put a mat at the foot of the mattress to cushion the descent.

## Horizontal Low Mirror

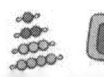

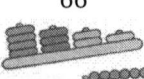

For proper development, it is important for the toddler to be able to see themselves and become aware of themselves. Place a low, horizontal shatterproof, and anti-shattering mirror in the nursery, so the toddler does not risk getting hurt. Thanks to the mirror, the toddler will have a global view of the room and be motivated to lift their head to look at their reflection. The mirror encourages the toddler to move around, so it would be wise to position it away from the bed, determining the rest time. As the toddler grows, the mirror can be turned vertically and placed next to a low wardrobe.

## Low Closet

According to the Montessori Method's principle of independence, the toddler should be free to choose his clothes and shoes. Therefore, it is necessary to make clothing accessible through a low closet within his reach. An open closet, very simple and without doors, would be preferable; it will then be sufficient to mount a rod to hang some clothes and a few shelves for folded garments. Select a few clothing items and place them in his small closet in rotation so he can choose them himself. Given the simplicity of the closet, you can also make it "DIY" by using wood panels or a low horizontal top and plastic tubing.

Near the closet, you can place a basket where the toddler can store clothes to be washed and also a small vertical mirror (you can use the horizontal one and turn it upside down) so that he can admire himself. You can also place a coat rack on the floor or wall so the little one can hang his coat, apron, and backpack.

## Small Chair

To help your toddler in the task of dressing himself, you can place a small chair next to the small closet that can be of support to him when he needs to put on pants or put on shoes. In this way, he will avoid sitting on the floor.

## Shelf with Storage Baskets

Of course, games must also be within the toddler's reach and should be placed in an orderly manner. A tidy environment will encourage the toddler to put everything back in its place. For this purpose, you can add baskets, plastic boxes, pull-out drawers, or low wooden boxes in the nursery to hold his toys.

But what are the learning materials to include in the nursery? In Part II of this book, you will find all the materials and activities you can offer your toddler. Choose materials according to age group and offer them in rotation.

## Carpet

Since toddlers like to sit on the floor, place a rug with a rich fabric in the play corner so it is also a tactile experience.

## Bookstore

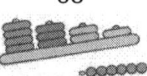

For the reading activity, add a small, low, open bookcase in the nursery with book supports that allow books to be placed front-to-back so that the toddler can recognize them immediately from the cover even though they cannot read. A small armchair or a small rug can also be placed nearby.

## Coffee Table and Small Chairs

Toddlers also need a space in which to let their creativity explode. Why not also include a small table and small chairs to accommodate friends? He can use them for drawing or role-plays, such as serving tea to dolls. You can also attach a paper roller to the table so that he can draw endlessly.

## Wall-mounted Blackboard

To stimulate your toddler's creativity even more (and prevent him from scribbling on the walls), you can apply chalkboard paint or rolls of chalkboard adhesive paper to the bottom strip of the walls. This way, he can give free rein to his imagination and clean it up by simply erasing it.

## Frames

You can decorate the walls with frames that allow you to insert and replace drawings made by your little one so they can be displayed as if they were works of art.

## Space for Imagination

There are times when the little one wants to relax and laze around; you can place large pillows in the nursery to allow him to be comfortable on the floor and on which he can read, draw and relax. When he grows up, you can think of a space that can be a kind of refuge and where he can feel free to dream; for example, you can place a small armchair or make a small hut, tent, or hammock.

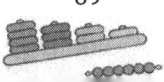

## Living Room

We will not dwell much on the living room because, by organizing the nursery as we have suggested, the toddler already has everything he needs in that room. However, you can also create a small comfortable space for him in the living room. Choose a spot near the window so that he can explore the outside world, enjoy the natural light, and mark it off with a rug. You can put a small table and seats on the rug; if you have not put it in the nursery, you can put the open bookcase in this small corner. You can also place containers like those in the nursery next to the small table so the toddler can store his items and materials and keep his small space tidy.

## Kitchen

The kitchen is an environment that is very attractive to children as it is where they see "making" and using their hands and where they often say, "I want to do it!" This environment, however, can be very dangerous. Let's see together how you can keep toddlers at your side and safe while they watch.

### Montessori Turret

The Montessori or learning tower is a very useful Montessori element in the kitchen. This stool allows toddlers to observe the activities taking place and participate in them in complete safety. It is a 1.20 m high wooden structure shaped like a tower and enclosed on three sides; the passageway with steps allows the toddler to climb up and down on their own and reach the work surface. From the tower, they can also knead and help the adults prepare the dishes. Of course, the adult's responsibility will be to keep them away from knives and stoves.

When your child gets too tall (ages 4 and up), you can replace the turret with the Montessori stool.

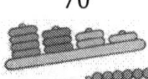

## Low Coffee Table

If space allows, you can also put a small table in the kitchen on which the child can work and knead.

## Custom-made Kitchen Apron

The apron is used to keep from getting dirty and plays a symbolic role; putting on an apron means starting to undertake an activity and doing it assiduously. Get your toddler an apron that he can wear himself and have him take it at the beginning of the activity and put it back in place at the conclusion.

## Toy Kitchen

A toy kitchen next to the coffee table can be very useful for teaching the toddler to organize space in the kitchen; he can store his small dishes, potholders, and dishcloths on the small shelves.

# Bathroom

## Grooming

As for the bathroom environment, if space allows, you can make a dressing table so that the little one can begin to understand the importance of personal care and get used to having a cleaning routine. The toddler can find his toothbrush, toothpaste, and towels in his little corner. It would also be helpful to have a small basin, but if that is not possible, you can place a turret or stool here so that he can use the basin independently.

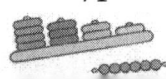

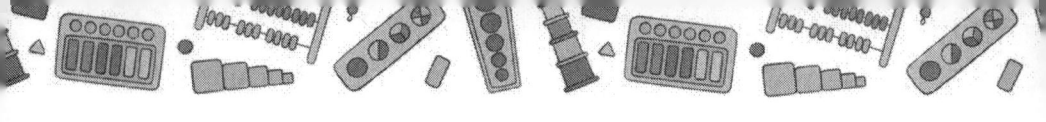

*Mirror*

The toddler should also be able to mirror himself in this environment. If it is impossible for you to place a mirror of their height, use the turret so they can follow their actions while doing personal care.

# Chapter 7: Montessori Activities in the Home.

In this chapter we will devote ourselves to proposing Montessori activities in the home. The activities are divided by category into stimulation, practical life, sensory, and developmental, and are classified in turn by age group; in this way, it will be very easy to identify the specific activities to propose to your toddler. Remember never to interrupt him when he is focused and absorbed. If you notice that despite his efforts, your toddler cannot perform the exercises correctly and does not learn from his mistakes, postpone the activity for a few weeks until he is ready; if, on the other hand, he is bored because he has a great mastery of the movements, increase the degree of difficulty or change the activity.

## STIMULATION ACTIVITIES

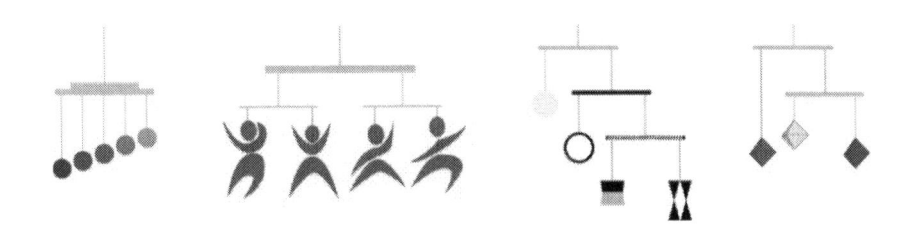

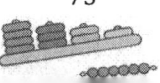

It's important to offer the toddler the right amount of stimulation: there should be neither too much nor too little. If you offer too many, he will not be able to focus his attention and will have difficulty concentrating; on the other hand, if there are too few, the toddler may become bored and consequently have crying fits because his needs are not being met. It's, therefore, necessary to be able to feed his curiosity without overstimulating him. The material proposed in this section aims to stimulate the toddler's curiosity and interest by working his mind and developing the ability to concentrate as early as the second week of life.

## From 0 to 5 Months

In the first 5 months, the baby develops the senses of sight and touch. In the beginning, sight is underdeveloped, and the baby can neither focus nor distinguish colors; this is precisely why Maria Montessori recommends using carousels or furniture at every stage of development. The carousels should be hung at a distance of 25 to 30 cm from the baby's face, which, by following the suspended objects, trains the mind and begins to get a feel for color, perception, and depth. To keep the baby's curiosity and attention alive, replacing the carousels every 2 to 3 weeks is necessary. It would be appropriate to introduce him to the first visual stimuli as early as the first 2 to 3 weeks of life. Since he cannot distinguish colors at this stage, it is necessary to start with Munari's merry-go-round, which consists of suspended objects in black and white. In subsequent weeks will use carousels with primary colors until he reaches the full scale of colors and shades.

### 1. Munari's Carousel

Purpose: To encourage concentration and enable the baby to focus on objects by observing shapes, contrasts, and proportion.

This suspended piece of furniture consists of very light elements that rotate slowly in the air around a central axis; the geometric paper shapes are in black and white, and there is a transparent sphere that reflects light.

Material:

- 3 wooden chopsticks (5mm in diameter)
- 1 white sheet and 1 black sheet
- 1 transparent sphere
- black and white paint

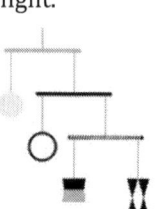

- Thread, glue, scissors, compass, ruler, pencil, paintbrush, and scotch tape

Cut the chopsticks into the following sizes: 36 cm, 30 cm, and 18 cm. Color the largest one white, the middle one black, and the small one black and white spiral. Create the geometric figures as in the picture and color them, then hang the decorated elements on the wands following the order in the picture.

## 2. The Carousel of Octahedra

Purpose: To stimulate the baby's vision by enabling him to learn and distinguish colors.

This hanging cabinet consists of a rod from which wires hang octahedra with the 3 primary colors.

Material:

- 1 wooden chopstick of 25 cm (7mm in diameter)
- Red, yellow and, blue sheets of matte or glossy paper
- thread, glue, scissors, ruler

Trace on the colored sheets the 3 octahedra (or download and print the shape from the web). Bend the edges and tape the wire together before closing it completely. Finally, tie the wires to the wand so that the octahedra result at different heights (with the blue being lower than the other colors). If you wish, you can make the octahedra different sizes. The larger blue (since it is the color the baby has a hard time distinguishing), the medium red, and the smaller yellow (it is the most visible color).

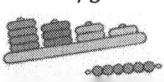

## 3. Gobbi's Carousel

Purpose: To develop visual sense by distinguishing shades.

The cabinet consists of 5 spheres in series with different shades of the same color. The spheres are covered with embroidery thread, aligned, and positioned upward.

Material:

- 1 drumstick 26cm long (5mm in diameter)
- 5 Styrofoam balls (4cm in diameter)
- 10 skeins of embroidery thread (2 for each shade)
- paint the same color as the darker sphere

Paint the wand with paint. Roll the embroidery thread around the orbs leaving extra thread. Hang the orbs by rolling the excess thread around the wand and being careful in the ladder arrangement. The darker sphere is the one that the baby has the most difficulty identifying, so it should be placed at the bottom, while the lighter sphere should be placed at the top.

## 4. The carousel of Dancers

Purpose: To increase the ability to concentrate and control voluntary arm movement.

This piece of furniture consists of 4 stylized shapes made of iridescent paper reflecting light and is 17 cm high. Each character is made up of parts that move independently, which gives the sense of movement and the impression that they are dancing.

Material:

- 3 wands 25, 30, and 35 cm long

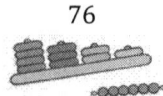

- Metallic or oleographic paper sheets with different color sides
- 1 spool of thread
- scissors and pencil

Draw the 4 dancers on the paper and cut out the patterns. Hang with string 2 dancers on the 25cm wand and 2 on the 30cm wand.

## 5. Suspended Objects

Purpose: stimulation of visual-motor skills.

By 4 months of age, the baby can perceive distances, has greater control of his arms, and can grasp objects more accurately. To meet his new need, you can offer him suspended objects that he can grasp; the object you choose should be strong and large enough and not be painted or varnished. You can suspend a ring or animal figures from a rubber band that will prompt the baby to reach out with his arms and hands toward them to touch them.

## 6. Rattles

Purpose: Stimulation of visual-motor skills, hearing, and eye-hand-ear coordination.

The rattle is also a suspended object, but unlike the others, it creates new stimuli for the baby. The sound produced by the movement of the rattle allows him to understand that it is the consequence of his movement. The rattle occurs only when the baby achieves his goal and creates gratification in him. This instrument also allows him to develop hand-finger coordination and thumb grip, which enables him to pick up small objects.

Material: offer the baby different rattles every two weeks with different materials, shapes, weights, colors, and temperatures.

## 7. The Sound Boxes

Purpose: stimulation of hearing.

Since the baby likes to grasp objects, you can create sound boxes and let him experience the sounds produced by the movement of each box.

Material:

- Small containers
- Dried lentils, pasta, or other
- Cloth bags

You can place objects that can reproduce a sound by shaking (such as dried lentils, pasta, or others) in very small containers (such as Kinder egg containers). Close the containers and place them in cloth bags of the same material and color. This way, the baby can focus only on the sound experience.

## 8. Music

Purpose: stimulation of hearing.

Listening to the right music can be a very relaxing experience for the baby. Choose calm tunes such as soft music, classical, chill out or lullabies, and disassociate this time from other activities so that the baby can focus solely on the sound experience.

## 9. Silence

Purpose: To stimulate concentration.

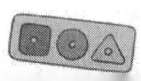

Silence helps the baby develop a strong ability to concentrate and a curiosity about sounds. Silence allows the isolation and highlighting of surrounding sounds and has a calming and soothing effect on the baby. Remember that silence is an achievement of babies and that overstimulating them is tantamount to not stimulating them. Therefore, allow your little one moments of silence.

## 10. Dressing up

Purpose: To stimulate collaboration.

When you dress your baby, communicate with him, describe what you are doing, and invite him to cooperate with phrases such as, "Push your little foot!"

## From 6 Months

## 11. Discovering New Flavors

Purpose: taste stimulation and autonomy.

Starting at 6 months, you can offer your baby new flavors such as water, compotes, baby food, and juices without added sugar. You can feed him with a small spoon until he can hold the cup with his own hands. Have him practice holding the spoon and bringing the feedings to his mouth. These times are great for encouraging autonomy.

## 12. Hide and Seek

Purpose: To stimulate visual ability.

As babies grow, they can follow objects with their eyes. You can then take advantage of this ability to hide objects under a napkin, partially and then completely. Ask a baby where the "missing" object is, lift the napkin, and encourage him to do the same.

## 13. Rhymes with Hands

Purpose: Acquisition of new words and space and temporal notions.

You can teach him nursery rhymes to learn the names of parts of the face or fingers. The words and rhythm will stick in the baby's memory.

## 14. Books

Purpose: To stimulate interest in discovery and reading.

Showing the baby books as early as infancy increases his desire to own them. Offer him cloth, cardboard, and paper books so that it can be a fantastic tactile experience for the little one. If you read them together, he will choose the ones he is most attracted to over time.

## 15. Animal Game

Purpose: To stimulate the ability to associate.

Name the animals for your baby and imitate their cries. He will learn to associate each verse with the corresponding animal.

## 16. Baskets

Purpose: Stimulation and development of hand coordination.

Put two or three objects in a small basket, such as a ball, a rattle, and a sound box. The baby will pick up the one he wants to handle. Replace the objects every two weeks; otherwise, he will get tired of the contents.

## 17. Activity Mat

Purpose: To stimulate concentration and perception of the concepts of space and boundary.

Provide the baby with a mat to carry out his activities. Working within a bounded space will promote his concentration, he will feel more secure and independent, and he will begin to perceive the concept of space.

## 18. The Boxes

Purpose: To develop hand-eye coordination.

The boxes allow the baby to acquire the notion of "object permanence" and experience the cause-and-effect relationship. The baby performs the movement guided by the mind and sees the effect.

You can buy or make many boxes out of wood or cardboard: one-shape, with geometric shapes, crocheted balls, and piggy banks. Each of these allows for activities that develop coordination as they grow from 6 months on. The box consists of a lid with a hole and a drawer. Once the box is made, simply change the lid by replacing it from time to time according to the difficulty.

First, familiarize him with the material before offering him the whole box, and then gradually increase the difficulty by presenting the box without the drawer and finally with the drawer.

## 19. Box with a Shape

Purpose: To develop hand-eye coordination.

Place the box with the round hole and the sphere on the activity mat but deprive it of the drawer. Very slowly, pick up the sphere and drop it into the hole in the box. The baby will observe the sphere's movement on the mat and replicate it.

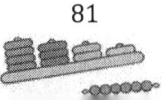

After the baby has developed a lot of manual dexterity with this activity, add the drawer to the box and give him the same exercise again by opening and closing the drawer to catch the ball.

## Since 9 Months

## 20. Eating Alone With Hands

Purpose: To encourage autonomy and discover new flavors.

In this age group, babies love to bring things to their mouths and taste everything. You can offer them whole pieces that they can munch on with their gums while always being very careful or small pieces of food. Foods that are already broken up train the baby's ability to grasp very small things with a pincer grip.

When you offer him new flavors, do not mix them with others; let the baby taste and associate that flavor with the food. Also, limit the use of salt and avoid sugar completely for at least 18 months; that way, he will be more attracted to fruits and vegetables.

## 21. Exploring in Freedom

Purpose: To improve motor skills.

As a baby begins to move, crawling and walking train his motor skills and tries to figure out how far he can go. While he is intent on discovering the environment around him, do not distract him or try to occupy him in other activities; you may cause him feelings of frustration.

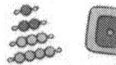

## 22. Containers and Caps

Purpose: Development of fine motor skills of the hand.

Material:

- Bottles and caps
- Box with lid

Choose different-sized bottles with matching caps. Cut out the lid of a box and create holes inside which to insert the bottles; this way, the bottles will remain stationary, and the baby will only have to worry about screwing and unscrewing the cap.

When he is proficient in this exercise, you can increase the difficulty by placing bottles with different-sized caps inside a basket; this way, he will not only have to screw and unscrew the caps but also have to learn to match the right caps to the containers.

## 23. Fill and Empty

Purpose: Visual-motor coordination and fine motor skills of the hand.

Material:

- Tray
- Small bowl with wooden washers
- Jar with lid

Present your baby with a tray on which you have placed a small bowl with wooden washers and a jar. He will need to practice pouring things inside the jar and closing and opening the lid. Through these movements, he can train fine hand motor skills and coordination.

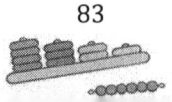

## 24. Basket of Treasures

Purpose: Stimulation of the five senses and language and development of hand coordination.

From 9 months onward, the baby needs to handle all the objects around him. Put the objects he sees him using daily in a basket and change them in rotation. You can include ladles, sponges, soft brushes, small glasses, and spoons (choose objects he cannot hurt himself with). You can then divide them by categories, such as putting together items used in the same environment, such as empty bottles, towels, brushes, ducks, etc., or glass, spoon, napkin, and ladle. In this way, he will learn to make associations with the environment. Help him learn their names by sitting with him and naming each object he picks.

## 25. Egg and Egg Holder

Purpose: To exercise hand muscles and coordination.

Material:

- Wooden egg and egg holder

The exercise consists of putting the wooden egg in the egg holder and taking it out. When the baby has mastered the movement, you can increase the difficulty of the exercise by replacing the egg with a ball.

## 26. Box with Geometric Shapes

Purpose: To stimulate and develop hand-eye coordination.

Unlike the previous one, the lid of this box has two holes with different geometric shapes. Always start by proposing one and then add the second to increase the difficulty. Start with the sphere, add the cube, then the prism, and so on.

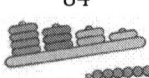

## 27. The Softball

Purpose: To develop hand-eye coordination and exercise the hand to push an object that offers resistance.

Line a Styrofoam ball with crochet thread or make it out of fabric and fill it with cotton. The size should be the same as the solid ball that the baby would push inside the box; it should also be soft but at the same time strong so that the baby will practice applying pressure to get it through the hole in the box.

## 28. Flat Grooves

Purpose: To stimulate visual-motor coordination.

Maria Montessori provided children with wooden jigs with geometric figures, on each of which was a knob. Through this activity, the baby practices pincer gripping with thumb and forefinger and improves coordination. Self-correction of the error enables him to improve his movements more and more by fitting the geometric shape perfectly in place.

### From 12 months

## 29. Learning the Parts of the Body

Purpose: To encourage autonomy.

Bath time is a great opportunity to teach your baby all the parts of the body and to encourage him to be independent and take care of his body. Provide him with a sponge and bubble bath and show him how to wash by always keeping the same sequence: first one arm, then the other, then the belly, then one leg, then the other, and so on; while you are showing him how to wash himself name all the body parts. For example, you can say, "Now let's wash the left arm," "Now let's wash the right leg," "the hair," and so on. It will stimulate his use of language, and in a short time, he will be able to name all parts of the body and even wash independently.

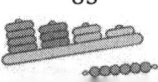

## 30. Reading Together

Purpose: To acquire new vocabulary, and develop listening and comprehension skills.

Let the toddler choose the book he prefers, even if only to flip through its pages; you do not have to read but just flip through the book with him and describe the pictures. You can ask him where a particular picture is, and he will point to it, or you can ask what picture it is, and he will have to tell you the name. If the toddler wishes, you can read the book with him; this way, he will have an enjoyable approach to reading.

## 31. Cubes on a Vertical Wand

Purpose: Stimulation and development of hand-eye coordination, concentration, and precision.

Material:

- Vertical wand
- Perforated cubes

Place the cubes on the activity mat and let the toddler become familiar with the material. Afterward, perform the exercise by sticking the perforated cubes into the wand. Repeat the gestures until the toddler begins to imitate them. Through repetition, he will practice the execution of the movement until he reaches perfection. Only at this point can you move on to the next exercise.

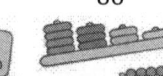

## 32. Discs on a Vertical Wand

Purpose: Stimulation and development of hand-eye coordination, concentration, and precision.

Material:

- Vertical wand
- Perforated discs

This exercise is similar to the previous one, but the grip is difficult. Unlike the cubes, grasping the discs is more complex for the toddler because he will have to practice pincer grasping between the thumb and the other fingers of the hand..

## 33. Discs on a Horizontal Rod

Purpose: Stimulation and development of hand-eye coordination, concentration, and precision.

Material:

- Horizontal wand
- Perforated discs

You can increase the difficulty of the previous exercise by arranging the discs on a horizontal stick. Always show the toddler how to do the activity and let him practice without disturbing or interrupting his flow of concentration. With repetition, he will reach perfection in his movements.

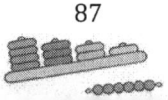

## 34. Colored Discs on Vertical Rods

Purpose: Stimulation and development of the ability to classify colors, concentration, and notions of quantities.

Material:

- 3 chopsticks of 3 different colors
- 9 discs (3 for each wand and the same color as the wand)

Unlike the previous exercises, this activity is done not with one but with three chopsticks. Before starting the exercise, place the material on the activity mat and let the toddler handle it to get familiar with it. After that, insert each colored disc into the wand of the corresponding color and let him continue. When he is finished, slip the discs out of the wands one by one, choosing one color at a time, and let the toddler do it again.

You can increase the difficulty of the exercise by using an abacus which allows you to reproduce the gestures accurately and learn the quantities.

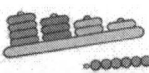

89

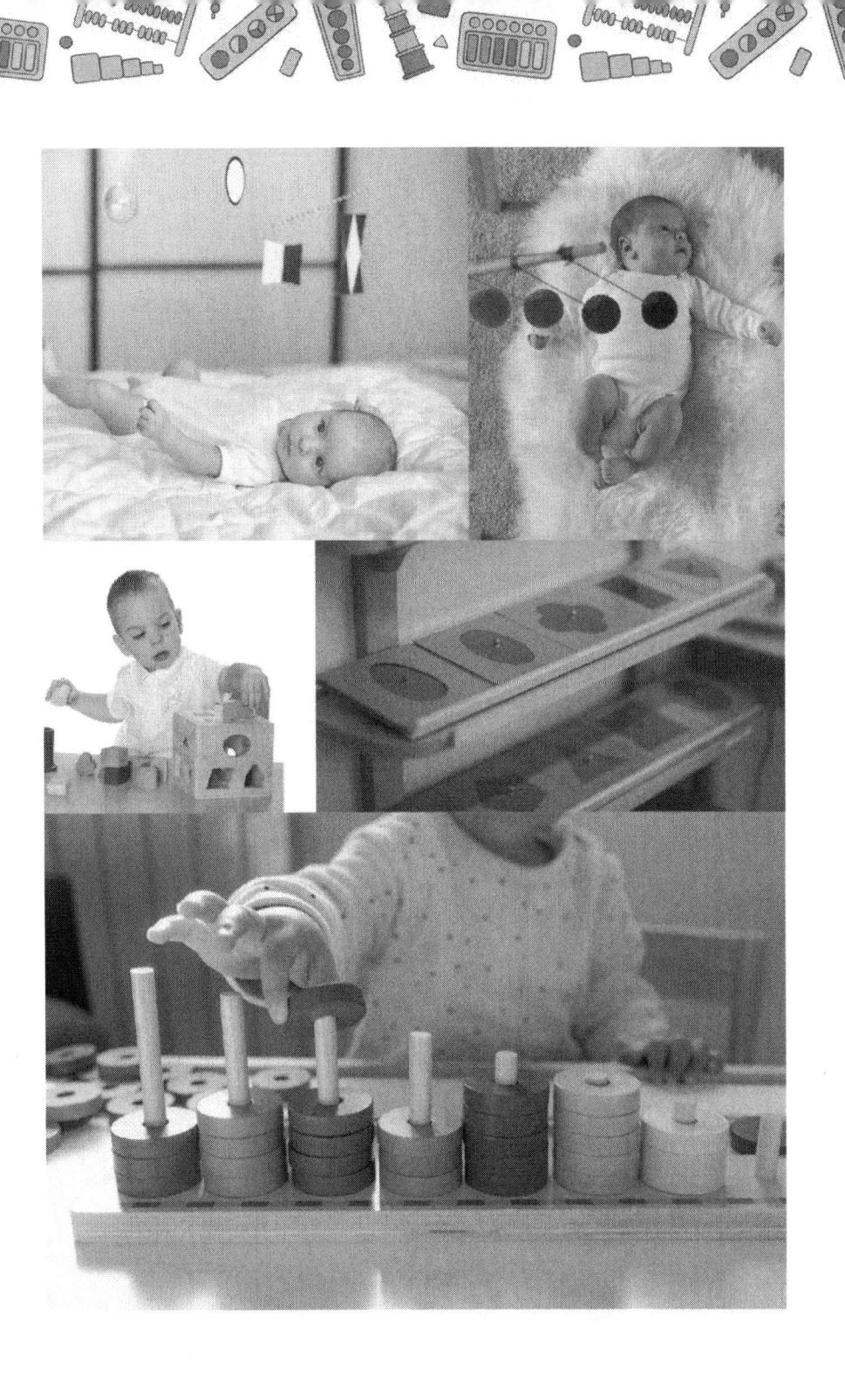

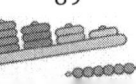

## PRACTICAL LIFE

The hands-on life activities begin at 12 months. In the previous months, you presented your baby with stimulation activities intended to prepare the little one for more difficult coordination activities. In this delicate age group, the toddler is no longer interested in playing but wants to use his hands and imitate adult activities. Therefore, allow him to practice activities and perfect his movements. Through practical life activities, the little one applies all the notions learned during stimulation activities; doing this requires a great deal of physical and mental work that allows him to develop additional skills, such as that concentration and control of his muscles, which are essential for achieving independence. It is also when the toddler builds his mind because he is completely absorbed in his actions. The practical life exercises proposed below aim to:

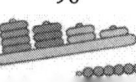

- Teach the importance of personal care and hygiene and acquire good habits;
- Learning to take care of the environment;
- Learning good manners;
- Perfecting the movements.

*From 12 months*

## 35. Manners

Purpose: To encourage the toddler to be kind to others.

Good manners are important in life. Encourage your toddler early on to say "Good morning" when he enters a room, store or finds friends; "Goodbye" when he leaves, or someone goes away; "Thank you" when he gets an answer to his requests; and "Please" when he has to ask for something. Repeat these "magic little words" often when you are with him, and in time he will learn to do it spontaneously.

## 36. The Pillow for Reflection

Purpose: To teach the toddler that it is important to respect rules and others. To create an atmosphere of peace and reflection and stimulate him to show empathy toward others.

The reflection pad is a great way to apply positive discipline when your toddler breaks the rules. If he has done something he should not have done, explain to him again why it is important to follow the rules and then have him sit on a reflective pad to reflect on his actions. Always speak calmly but at the same time in firm tones; after a few minutes, go to him and propose a solution (such as apologizing to someone); Finally, cuddle him so as not to undermine his self-esteem and make him understand that you are not angry with him.

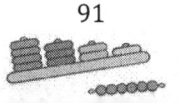

## 37. Eating Alone

Purpose: To promote autonomy, development of visual motor coordination, strength dosage, and achievement of balance.

Give your toddler a small fork, spoon, and knife so he can experiment with using them. Also, give him a napkin and show him how to clean himself after eating. As he practices the movements, he will be able to use the cutlery perfectly and pour water into the glass; he will be able to do everything very carefully and calmly without dropping anything. All these movements and their success will boost your toddler's self-esteem and motivate him to want to do it himself without any help.

## 38. Carrying Objects

Purpose: Development of motor skills, concentration skills, and autonomy.

Although it may seem easy, carrying an object requires a great deal of concentration on the toddler, who must coordinate his movements and hold what he has in his hands firmly so that he does not drop it all the way. To begin, you can ask him to carry objects such as a small plate or glass and hold them firmly in his hands. When he has gained confidence with this movement, you can increase the difficulty by asking him to carry a plate with food inside or a glass full of water; this way, he will learn to keep the plate and glass straight and not drop the contents.

These small activities may seem simple, but in reality, they are very complex because they require maximum concentration on the part of the toddler, who must gain gradual self-confidence, maintain balance, watch what they are carrying, and pay attention to obstacles without getting distracted along the way.

## 39. Carrying a Tray

Purpose: To increase precision skills, coordination, concentration, and autonomy.

If your toddler has already practiced carrying objects such as plates, glasses, and empty trays, you can increase the difficulty of the exercise by placing an object inside the tray and asking him to carry it. This activity allows him to tell immediately if he is making a mistake in the movement because the object inside the tray will move or fall. When he has mastered this movement and can carry the tray without tilting it and keeping the objects perfectly still, you can increase the difficulty again by having him carry a glass with water inside the tray. With a little practice, he will be able to carry his breakfast and snack into the tray, increasing his self-esteem and sense of independence.

## 40. Use of Sponge

Purpose: To foster autonomy, development of hand-eye coordination and concentration, and learn the first concepts of fluid absorption.

As simple as it may seem, using the sponge is a fairly complex activity for your toddler. He must first learn how to pick it up correctly, observe how the sponge can absorb water, and finally learn that it is necessary to wring it out to get the liquid out.

Material:

- Tray
- Sponge
- A basin full of water
- Empty basin

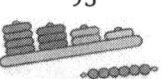

Place the two basins on the tray, the left full of water and the right empty. Show the toddler how to soak the sponge with water in the first basin and then wring it out in the empty one. Toddlers like to play with water. Let your toddler practice movement; he will learn not only how to coordinate his movements and concentrate but also how to be autonomous because he will be able to remedy his mistakes (if he drops to water, the toddler will be perfectly able to use the sponge to clean it up); he will also master the left-to-right movement useful for the future writing activity.

## For 15 months

### 41. Washing Hands

Purpose: To foster autonomy and instill good habits.

Teach your toddler how to wash his hands by rubbing his fingers first, then between his fingers, then the back, and finally the palm. Show them how to rinse them well so that no soap residue is left behind, and finally, how to dry them. Make washing his hands a habit and encourage him to do it often, such as when he comes back into the house, between activities, before eating, after doing his business, etc.

### 42. Brushing Teeth

Purpose: To foster autonomy and self-care.

Explain to your toddler that brushing his teeth is very important. When he sees that you brush them regularly, he will have the desire to imitate you and will want his toothbrush. Make a small toothbrush and toothpaste available to him so that he can take it to do his activity, and explain that you only need to use a very small amount of toothpaste. Show him how to clean his teeth with slow gestures: front, back, top, and bottom. When finished, he can put the toothbrush away and dry himself with the towel. It is an excellent opportunity to create a routine in his mind and involve him in such an important activity as personal hygiene care. You can also take this opportunity to expand his vocabulary by naming all the teeth: molars, canines, etc.

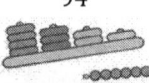

## 43. Dressing Yourself

Purpose: To foster autonomy.

If you have followed the instructions in this book for creating a toddler-friendly bedroom, now is the time to encourage him to choose his clothes from the few items you have arranged in the small closet. Show him how to dress and encourage him to practice buttoning and unbuttoning. This learning process will take a long time but do not help him or dress him yourself. The little one must learn how to do it himself and that he has a mirror to check that everything is in order before he leaves the room.

## 44. Putting Clothes Away

Purpose: To foster autonomy.

Show your toddler how to fold his pants, socks, and shirts and how to store each one in its drawer. Also, teach him how to hang up his backpack, apron, and jacket every time he comes home; this way, he will learn how to keep his things tidy.

## 45. Preparing Clothes for the Next Day

Purpose: To increase a sense of responsibility and autonomy.

Another way to foster your toddler's autonomy is to help him prepare clothes for the next day; this will increase his sense of responsibility and organizational skills as he learns to prepare for the next day. You can also use this time to help your child enrich his vocabulary by naming everything he picks up, such as sweaters, socks, shirts, pants, etc.

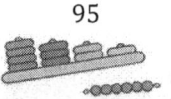

## 46. Making Needs

Purpose: To foster autonomy.

Take advantage of the toddler's psychic period of 12 to 18 months to teach him to use the toilet. Place a small potty in the corner of the bathroom and invite him regularly to sit after meals and before going to bed or going out so that habits are created. Observe him and try to figure out at what times to offer him a little bathroom break. Very soon, the little one will ask to go to the bathroom when he feels needed until he becomes fully autonomous.

## 47. Passing the Sponge

Purpose: To foster independence, to teach the toddler to take care of himself and his surroundings.

After you have taught your toddler to use the sponge, you can teach him to use it to clean. Do not force him to do this but present it to him as a fun activity; in this way, he will willingly clean and keep his surroundings tidy.

## 48. Dusting

Purpose: To learn how to care for the environment and cooperate in household activities.

Show the toddler how the furniture fills with dust, then teach him how to dust and give him a feather duster so he can imitate your movements. Remember that the toddler is watching you very carefully, so when you dust, try to be as precise as possible: lift all the objects on the furniture and then dust. By observing this, the toddler will be motivated to do the same to imitate you precisely.

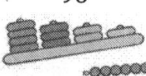

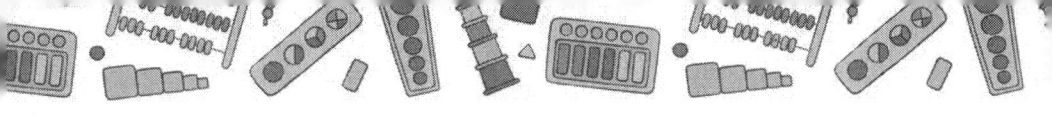

## 49. Learning to Use the Knife

Purpose: Visual-motor coordination, fosters autonomy.

Material:

- Vegetable
- Cutting board
- Knife
- Plate

When your toddler has learned to use the wavy-bladed vegetable cutter, you can offer him a round-tipped knife to cut soft foods such as bananas. Have him hold the knife with one hand while pushing with the other.

Place the cutting board on the coffee table, then place the vegetable on the left side of the cutting board and the plate on the right side. In this way, the toddler will take the vegetable from the left and place it on the cutting board to the right; then, after cutting with the knife, he will place the vegetable slices on the plate to his right. This activity develops his motor and cognitive skills and prepares him for future writing activities by performing movements from left to right.

When he has mastered the knife, you can put a potato peeler at his disposal.

## 50. Spread

Purpose: Visual-motor coordination, fosters autonomy.

Provide the toddler with a butter knife, show him how to spread cream cheese on a slice of bread, and let him do it himself. This way, the toddler will practice performing the movement and will be able to prepare a snack or breakfast on his own.

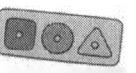

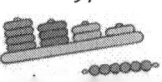

## 51. Preparing the Snack

Purpose: To foster autonomy and the ability to choose.

You can use snack time to teach your toddler to be independent. If you can, reserve a small shelf in the lower part of the kitchen where you can put his dishes, placemat, and healthy snacks, then do the same with the refrigerator. This way, you will decide what your toddler eats, but he will choose what he eats at that time. If he has already learned to spread with a knife, he may make a jam sandwich, take some fruit from the bottom shelf of the refrigerator and peel it himself, or a yogurt. In this way, while you will be reassured that his choice will fall on healthy and wholesome foods, his self-esteem, autonomy, and ability to choose will increase.

## 52. Squeeze the Citrus Fruit

Purpose: To practice acquired skills, develop concentration ability, visual motor coordination, balance, strength, and foster independence.

Material:

- Tray
- Juicer
- Orange and lemon halves
- 1 glass
- 1 sponge

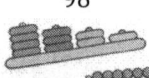

Before offering this activity, ensure that your toddler has already acquired the skills to do so by practicing decanting and using the sponge; if they are already very proficient at this, you can take it to the next level by allowing them to squeeze citrus fruits. Always use a tray to place the juicer, orange and lemon halves, a glass, and a sponge. Show the toddler how to hold the juicer firmly with the left hand, place one half of the orange, and perform the motion to squeeze it with the right hand. This activity gives toddlers a lot of satisfaction as they see the juice pouring out. When he is finished, ask him to pour the juice into the glass and wipe off any splashes with the sponge. He can squeeze the other half of the orange or the lemon half at this point. Once he has mastered the motion, he can decide to prepare juice for snacking.

## 53. Grate

Purpose: To develop fine motor skills, visual-motor coordination, and rhythm perception and promote autonomy.

Get the toddler a sturdy square grater. Show him how to perform the activity by grating **only** from top to bottom. This way, the gesture will be easier to understand and safer when replicated. The toddler can then enjoy different grating foods such as cheese, bread, carrots, apple, etc.

## 54. Pass

Purpose: To develop fine motor skills, visual-motor coordination, and rhythm perception, and promote autonomy.

Material:

- Cooked vegetables or fruit
- Masher
- Empty bowl

Another way to get toddlers practice cooking is to pass vegetables inside a vegetable masher. Remember always to put the vegetables to be mashed to the left and the empty bowl to the right. As toddlers perform they work with utmost concentration, they will practice the same movement as writing. Once the task is finished, they can enjoy eating the vegetable or fruit puree.

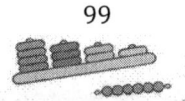

## 55. Pounding

Purpose: to calibrate force, coordinate gestures, and learn the succession of movements.

Material:

- Pestle
- Mortar

Show your toddler the different movements: tapping, squeezing, and rotating. Once learned, show him how to perform them in succession. He can crush spices and dried fruits and make basil pesto when he has mastered the technique.

## 56. Washing Dishes

Purpose: Visual-motor coordination, fosters autonomy.

Material:

- Montessori turret
- Apron
- Sponge
- Dishcloth

With the help of the Montessori tower, you can teach your toddler to wash dishes. Invite him to put on his apron, then fill the left basin of the sink with water and some soap and the right basin with just water. Place the items on the left side of the basin with soap, then show the toddler how to wash them. He should take one at a time, dip it in the water with soap, wash it with the sponge, rinse it in clean water, and then place it on the dish rack. This activity allows him to improve his movements and prepares him for future writing activities. After washing all the dishes, he can empty the tubs and clean them with a sponge. Finally, show him how to dry the dishes with a dishcloth and how to put them away in the cupboards. Washing, drying, and putting dishes away is a rewarding activity for the toddler and teaches him to complete a task from start to finish.

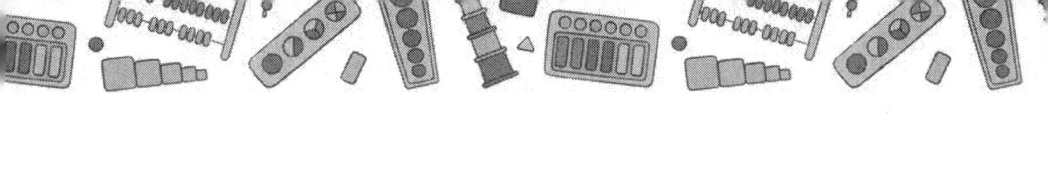

## 57. Stow the Socks

Purpose: To develop concentration and satisfy the need for order.

While folding clean laundry, let your toddler sort the socks and pair them up. This activity satisfies his need for order and allows him to stay focused by trying to spot the two matching socks and then pair them up. After pairing them up, he can put them back in the corresponding drawers.

## 58. Sorting the Dishes

Purpose: To select and classify objects and satisfy the need for order.

When you wash the dishes, let the toddler rearrange them in the drawer; this way, he can accomplish an activity that greatly satisfies him and simultaneously make himself useful. To sort them and put them in the right place, he will first have to find the similarities and figure out to which category they belong. Should he make a mistake, remember not to take him back and especially not to interrupt him. During an activity, his concentration is highest. Let him make mistakes and learn from his mistakes.

## 59. Setting the Table

Purpose: To develop coordination and perfect movements.

Teach your toddler to set his little table by providing him with fabric placemats on which he can place plates, cutlery, and glasses. He will then learn to recognize all the items on the table and to take them from the cupboard by himself. When he learns to set his little table, you can increase the difficulty of this useful household activity by giving him the task of setting the "grown-up table."

## 60. Cleaning the Table

Purpose: To become familiar with large movements and to complete a task.

Dip a sponge into the water and show the toddler how to clean the table; be meticulous in doing this because the toddler will watch you carefully and try to replicate the movements as precisely as possible. After he has wiped the sponge all over the surface, edges, and corners, provide him with a dry cloth and encourage him to wipe by performing the same motion.

## 61. Doing Laundry

Purpose: To develop fine motor skills of the hand.

Lay a clothesline at the toddler's height, or get a baby clothesline. Put in a basket the laundry that the little one can take, such as handkerchiefs, socks, panties, and tea towels, and get him some clothespins that he can open easily. Show him how to hang them, and let him practice doing it himself. This activity will not only allow him to develop fine motor skills in his hand but will also boost his self-esteem and his willingness to help you with household chores.

## 62. Cleaning Glasses

Purpose: To improve coordination and execution of large movements.

Teaching your toddler to clean glass is a good activity to perform large movements and to work the body muscles. Provide him with a spray bottle and rag and show him the movement to perform on the glass. Stand beside him but let him learn on his own. If he sprays too much liquid, it will fall on the floor, and he will realize his mistake and try to fix it; if, on the other hand, he forgets to wipe or wipes poorly, the glass will be full of stains. The more the toddler practices repeating this activity, the more he will notice his mistakes.

## 63. Grocery Shopping

Purpose: To involve the child in daily activities.

Try to convey to your toddler the importance of grocery shopping, explain its purpose, and involve him in activities that he can also do, such as putting change in the cart, carrying the small cart, putting things in it, and getting tickets to the departments. Remember, however, that the supermarket is a source of stress for the little one because it is full of people, very bright lights, and music. Try to distract him from all this by engaging him in activities within his reach, but if he gets nervous, try to keep calm. Do not blackmail him or offer him something in return; otherwise, he will be led to think that behaving well means he deserves a reward, and as a result, he will try to get something from you every time you shop.

## 64. Harvesting Fruits and Vegetables

Purpose: Contact with nature and discovery of the world around him, development of fine hand movement, precision, concentration, and coordination.

Suppose you have a chance to plant seeds with your toddler and show him how they turn into plants, how fruits grow on trees, in bushes, or on the ground, and even how they are harvested. These will be growing moments for him, and in his mind, he will elaborate on developing and harvesting plants.

Show him how to pick mushrooms, strawberries, apples from trees, herbs, etc. Picking small fruits requires great concentration on the part of the toddler and pincer grasping skills. He must also be careful to gently perform his gestures so as not to spoil the fruit. Take time to spend these pleasant moments with him, and you will see the satisfaction in his eyes when he eats the fruit of his labor: what he has very carefully picked with his little hands.

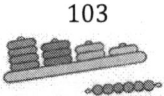

## 65. Taking Care of a Plant

Purpose: Learn to care for other life forms.

Material:

- Small watering can
- Small sprayer
- Sponge

Give your toddler the task of caring for a specific plant within the house. When he sees that you take care of the plants, he will want to do the same to imitate you. Show him how to pour water into the plant's soil, spray the leaves, and provide him with a sponge to dry it if he spills it on the floor. Show him how to remove dried leaves or flowers and do this activity always together to instill in his love and respect for other life forms.

## 66. Making Lasagna and Pizza

Purpose: To grasp a sense of rhythm, order, and proportion.

Toddlers like to watch but especially like to imitate and help adults in their activities. You can involve them in activities in the kitchen and prepare meals together with them. For example, if you are making a lasagna or pizza, why not include them in activities such as distributing sauces and toppings? Distributing sauces with the help of a spoon, sprinkling salt and oregano, or putting in the right amounts of mozzarella, ham, and olives requires a lot of effort, concentration, and precision. When the toddler is immersed in these activities, in addition to feeling useful and increasing his self-esteem, he learns rhythm and proportion; he will also learn how to repair his damage (should he accidentally drop something or make a mess) and how to clean up while maintaining order.

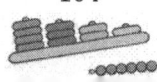

105

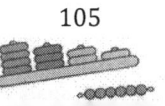

## SENSORY ACTIVITIES

The child understands the world around him through the 5 senses through which he acquires new information and connects what the toddler already knows with what he learns. Because sight, touch, hearing, smell, and taste are used, the baby is immersed in sensory activities as early as the first months of life and experiences them independently.

Maria's Method is based precisely on what the child learns for himself, and these discoveries are mainly the result of the experience made by the senses; in this regard, she said:

> "Observers are not created by saying: observe: but by giving the means to observe: and these means are the education of the senses. Once that relationship between the child and the 'environment is established, progress is assured, for the refined senses lead to the better observation of the 'environment,' and this, with its

*varieties attracting attention, continues the sensory education."* [24]

The activities offered in this section are intended to provide the toddler with the means to observe the environment while leaving him free to progress at his own pace.

## From 6 Months

### 67. Tactile Pillows

Purpose: To stimulate tactile perception.

The baby discovers different fabrics by touch through pillows that you can make yourself using different fabrics (cotton fabrics, wool, silk, satin, jute, felt, tulle, etc.) but of the same color so that he can focus only on one characteristic: the diversity of the material. You can then place these fabrics inside a box and offer a tactile experience to the baby. Alternatively, you can use the fabrics to create small cotton-filled pillows.

### 68. Rag Puppet

Purpose: To stimulate tactile perception by experimenting with textures.

Material:

- Fabric
- Needle
- Wire
- Scissors
- Wadding
- Ribbons

---

[24] M.MONTESSORI, *The Discovery of the Child,* Garzanti, Milan, 1970, 185.

- Threads of wool
- Tassels

Draw two identical animal silhouettes on the fabric and cut them out. Sew the two silhouettes together and fill them with absorbent cotton. Decorate the puppet as you like by placing woolen threads, ribbons, etc. Avoid going overboard with decorations, especially do not insert small elements your baby might swallow, such as buttons.

## 69. First Racking

Purpose: Refinement of fine hand movement.

Ostensibly pouring may seem like a simple activity, but in reality, it stimulates intellectual development and many skills, such as hand-eye coordination, self-control, and remarkable hand skills. Decanting can be offered to the baby in different age groups and with different materials, but it would be wise to start with safe materials that he can neither swallow nor inhale.

Material:

- Unbreakable glass, wooden, or metal containers
- Pasta, beans, wooden blocks, etc.

Offer him a container and the material to put inside. Then, when he has become familiar with it, and you feel he is ready to decant, give him another container, the same as the first, so that he can move objects from one container to the other. When the object falls, it will produce noise and allow the baby to correct his mistakes and perfect his movements.

## 70. Finger Painting

Purpose: To understand the effects of its movements and the concept of cause-and-effect.

Material:

- Large drawing sheet
- Colors that are non-toxic, washable, and not dangerous if put in the mouth

Place the 3 primary colors directly on the sheet and let your baby use his hands and feet, experience the feel of the color on his skin, and see with his own eyes the colorful consequences of his actions. You can do this activity again when he is older by using sheets of paper hung on a washable wall or an easel.

## Since 9 Months

## 71. The Sensory Panels

Purpose: To stimulate tactile perception.

Material:

- Thick cardboard
- Sandpaper, knurled adhesive paper, soft plastic, cork, wood, styrofoam, sponge, velvety fabric, carpet, etc.

Cut the different materials, so they are all the same size (30x30cm), then stick them on thick cardboard to make panels. Place the panels on the ground, let the baby play with them, and discover the different features. When the baby is older, he can walk on them barefoot and have a different sensory experience.

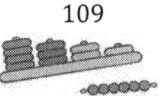

## 72. The Colorful Bags

Purpose: To learn to distinguish primary colors and expand vocabulary.

Material:

- 3 cloth bags of the primary colors (red, yellow, and blue)
- Objects of primary colors

Place objects of the same color inside the bags, then present the baby with one bag at a time and its contents, telling him what it is and also what color it is; in this way, he will learn to distinguish colors and associate them with objects. When he has become familiar, ask him to sort the objects by color and put them back into the corresponding bag.

## 73. The Colored Sticks

Purpose: To learn to distinguish colors.

Material:

- Colored glasses or covered with colored paper
- Wooden sticks of different colors

Present the materials to your baby, ask them to sort the sticks by color, and place them in the respective small jar of the same color. Start with the primary colors red, yellow, and blue. When your little one is familiar with and can recognize the primary colors perfectly, you can increase the difficulty of the exercise by adding other colors.

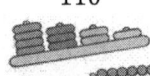

## 74. Tooled Decanting

Purpose: Refinement of fine hand movement.

You can increase the difficulty of decanting by adding utensils such as a spoon.

Material:

- 2 containers or bowls made of unbreakable glass, ceramic, or metal
- pasta, beans, lentils, etc.
- 1 tablespoon

Arrange the two containers on a small table. Fill the left container with the material you have chosen, then show the baby the exercise by explaining verbally what you are doing. Using a spoon, take the material from the left bowl and pour it into the right one with very slow, repetitive movements, then invite the little one to do the same. Using the spoon will enable him to gain confidence in his movements and to practice handling the cutlery; also, the movement from left to right prepares him for the writing activity.

## 75. Decanting With Water

Purpose: refinement of fine hand motion. First notions of liquid incompressibility.

When the baby has become familiar with solid decants, you can increase the difficulty of the exercise by changing materials and offering liquid ones.

Materials:

- 1 jug full of water
- 1 glass
- 1 sponge

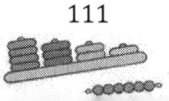

Place the material on a tray and show the little one how to decant the water from the pitcher into the glass, then invite him to do it himself. He will learn how much to fill the glass at his own expense: if he fills it too much, the water will spill out. Show him how to use the sponge so he can fix his own mistakes.

## From 12 Months

## 76. Heuristic Game

Purpose: Development of concentration and manipulative skills.

Heuristic play is a more complex development of the treasure basket and involves offering the toddler a jute or cotton sack filled with more than 40 objects to manipulate belonging to different categories and closed by a string. Place it on the activity mat along with three bowls, then let the toddler open the sack and place materials in order on the mat after studying them carefully.

## 77. Bag of Mysteries

Purpose: To develop a tactile sense and recognition of shapes and objects.

Material:

- Cloth bag
- Objects of various kinds

Place various objects inside a cloth bag and give the bag to the toddler. Have him take one object at a time and invite him to manipulate it so that he can figure out what object it is without looking at it. Ask him to name the object and take it out of the bag to see if he has figured out what object it is.

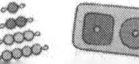

## 78. Perfecting Decanting

Purpose: To foster independence and development of hand-eye coordination and concentration skills.

As your toddler grows, you can increase the difficulty of the transfers so that he can perfect his movements.

Material:

- Tray
- 2 bowls
- 1 teaspoon
- 2 bottles
- 1 funnel

Always delimit the toddler's space for action with a tray inside which you can add two bowls: the one on the left should be filled with small materials such as lentils or flour, while the one on the right will remain empty. Provide him with a small spoon to increase the difficulty of the exercise and let him transfer the material from the left bowl to the right one. If he drops something from the teaspoon, he will realize his mistake and work on perfecting his movement.

You can increase the difficulty of the exercise by placing two bottles inside the tray: one full of water and the other empty. Provide the little one with a funnel and show the toddler how to decant water into an empty bottle. This activity is very difficult for the toddler because he has to be able to hold the full bottle firmly in his hand so that it does not fall out, and at the same time, he has to give it full concentration so that he can coordinate his movements and control the flow of the liquid so that it does not spill out of the funnel.

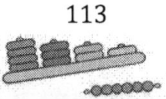

## 79. The Pink Tower

Purpose: To train visual motor coordination, learn to recognize magnitudes and the difference between large and small, and understand the physical basis of the balance.

The pink tower consists of 10 wooden cubes of precise size and colored pink. The smallest cube at the base is 1 cm, while the largest measures 10 cm. Through manipulation, the toddler learns to recognize the different sizes; you can help him by showing him which cube is the largest and which is the smallest. The toddler will then experience balance by stacking the cubes; when they fall, the toddler will start over and continue his exercise by trying to balance them.

## 80. Chess

Purpose: To distinguish colors by dividing whites from blacks, flatten similar but differently colored figures, and flatten the same ones.

Chess is very versatile in allowing the toddler to develop different skills. Let the toddler manipulate the chess figures by becoming familiar with them; then, you can propose that he separate the whites from the blacks; later, you can increase the difficulty of the exercise by asking him to place each checkmate on the chess board square of the same color. You can, for example, invite him to find all similar figures and separate them by placing them inside small boxes. Chess is very versatile, so you can use it in different age groups by proposing activities with different degrees of difficulty and increasing the level from time to time.

## 81. Model

Purpose: To develop creativity and manipulative skills.

Toddlers love to knead and shape. To satisfy this need of theirs and allow them to express their creativity, you can come up with plasticine, clay, Das, salt dough, pizza dough, etc. Plasticine has great potential for manipulation, and you can make it together with your toddler using the following materials.

Material:

- 2 tablespoons of lemon juice
- ½ cup cornstarch
- 1 cup of boiling water
- ½ cup fine salt
- 2 cups of flour
- 2 tablespoons of oil
- Food coloring or spices (saffron, turmeric, cocoa, paprika)

Mix the dry ingredients, then add the liquid ingredients and knead. Divide the dough into balls, add a different food coloring or the spices of your choice, and knead. The plasticine is ready for your toddler to use.

Alternatively, you can make salt dough, create beautiful shapes, and air dry them. Once they have hardened, your toddler can decorate them with tempera or acrylic paints. You can also use clay, or if you make pizza or bread dough, give them pieces of dough and let them play with it.

## For 15 Months

### 82. The Perfume Boxes

Purpose: To educate the sense of smell.

Material:

- Small glass containers
- Spices and herbs

Fill each small container with a different spice (paprika, cumin, curry, turmeric, nutmeg, saffron, salt, pepper, etc.) and let the toddler smell and taste them. If you have a chance, plant aromatic herbs such as basil, mint, marjoram, rosemary, parsley, thyme, etc., with him; not only will he be able to observe their growth and drying, but he will also be able to realize the physical and olfactory differences of each aromatic herb. When you cook, use spices, tell the toddler which spice it is and let him smell the scents of the different preparations. The scents will create a permanent imprint in the toddler's mind, who will not only remember them in his memory for a lifetime but will also be able to associate each scent with the corresponding spice or aromatic herb.

### 83. Discovering New Flavors

Purpose: To refine taste.

In addition to sharpening the sense of smell, you can also use spices to sharpen the sense of taste. Use spices in cooking and show your toddler how they change and improve food taste. For example, you can add curry to chicken, paprika or turmeric to potatoes, nutmeg to mashed potatoes, ginger to bananas, etc. Allow him to train his taste to recognize which spices have been used to prepare dishes.

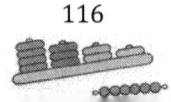

## 84. Fruit Tasting

Purpose: To match a taste to each fruit, observe and identify differences, and enrich vocabulary.

Show your toddler the whole fruits and, taking them one at a time, tell him what they are called. Then dwell on their characteristics: whether they have a skin or no skin, whether they have seeds or a stone inside, whether they taste sweet or sour, and what kind of fragrance they give off; open them and study them with him, then have him practice cutting the fruit with his small knife. Each time he cuts a different fruit, have him taste it and repeat the name of the fruit so that he can associate the taste with the name of the fruit. You can make this activity even more fun by creating fruit salad cups; each time he catches a piece of fruit, he can try to figure out which fruit it is through sight and taste.

## 85. Screws and Bolts

Purpose: Development of hand fine motor skills and concentration skills.

Material:

- Tray
- Screws with their respective bolts

In a tray, put different-sized screws with their bolts and arrange them in order of size. Take the smallest screw and show the toddler how to screw it into its bolt, then let him do it himself. By practicing this activity, the toddler will develop strong concentration skills, improve his thumb and forefinger pincer grip, and perfect the movement of screwing and unscrewing.

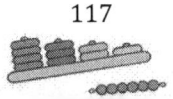

## 86. Painting with a Brush

Purpose: To train grip, control the fine movement of the hand, and observe the consequences of one's actions.

Material:

- Temperas
- Watercolors of the 3 primary colors (red, yellow, and blue)
- 1 short coarse-headed brush
- Sheets of coarse-grained paper
- 1 small bowl

Painting with a brush allows the toddler to observe how each movement corresponds to a colored line, larger or smaller depending on the pressure applied, that follows his hand. Using only the primary colors also allows him to see how they combine to create other colors. Leave the material available for him to experiment on his own.

## From 18 Months

## 87. Sound Memory

Purpose: To sharpen the sense of hearing, concentration, attention, and memory.

Material:

- 6 small wooden boxes
- 2 different colors
- Small materials (rice, pasta, beans, bells, screws, glass marbles, etc.)

Take small boxes and color three lids of one color and three of another. Place materials of different types inside the small boxes of the first color that, when shaken, cause different and distinguishable sounds between them; then, put the same materials inside the small boxes of the second color. Close the small boxes tightly and shake them next to the toddler's ear, explaining the difference between loud and soft. At this point, divide the small boxes by color by putting all the boxes of the first color on the left and all the boxes of the second color on the right. Then take a little box from the left and shake it, then have the toddler take a little box from the right and ask if it makes the same sound. If the sound is the same, the toddler can put the two little boxes of different colors side by side. Otherwise, he will continue looking for the little box that makes the same sound as the other. When the toddler is familiar with the activity, has honed his sense of hearing, and can recognize the three sounds, you can increase the difficulty of the exercise by adding more small boxes with different materials inside.

## From 2 Years

## 88. The Scissors

Purpose: Development of concentration and fine motor skills of the hand.

Material:

- Strips of cardboard
- Scissors

Don't be afraid to teach your toddler how to use scissors. Have him sit in his little coffee table chair, stand behind him, and show him how to put his fingers in the scissors correctly. Have him practice opening and closing the scissors without cutting anything. When he has correctly grasped the scissors with his right hand, hold the card firmly and allow him to practice cutting. When he gains confidence in the movement, you can have him hold the cardstock in his left hand and offer to cut on his own.

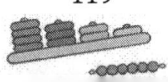

## 89. Glue

Purpose: Development of concentration and fine motor skills of the hand.

Material:

- Pieces of cardboard
- Glue stick
- Liquid glue
- Brush

After your toddlers have practiced cutting strips of cardstock and cutting out small pieces, you can show them how to use glue sticks. Create a circle on a sheet of paper and have your little one stick the cut-out pieces inside it. He will need to take the paper pieces, place them on the glue, and then glue them inside the circle (alternatively, you can show the children how to use liquid glue with the help of a brush). When they have become familiar with this activity, you can increase the difficulty of the exercise by creating figures such as squares or triangles, inside which they will stick the paper pieces. Once these cutting and gluing skills are improved, you can carry out many decoupage activities with the toddlers.

*For 2 1/2 Years*

## 90. Decant With Tongs

Purpose: To refine hand fine motor skills, precision, and visual-motor coordination.

Material:

- Tray
- 2 bowls
- 1 plier
- Large and small objects (nuts, glass marbles, olives, beads, etc. )

Put the two small bowls in the tray; into the left one, insert the objects starting with the larger ones, while the right bowl should be empty. Give the toddler a pair of tongs and show him how to decant the objects into the empty bowl. The left-to-right movements in this exercise will also prepare him for the writing activity. When he has become familiar with it, you can replace the large objects with smaller ones.

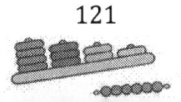

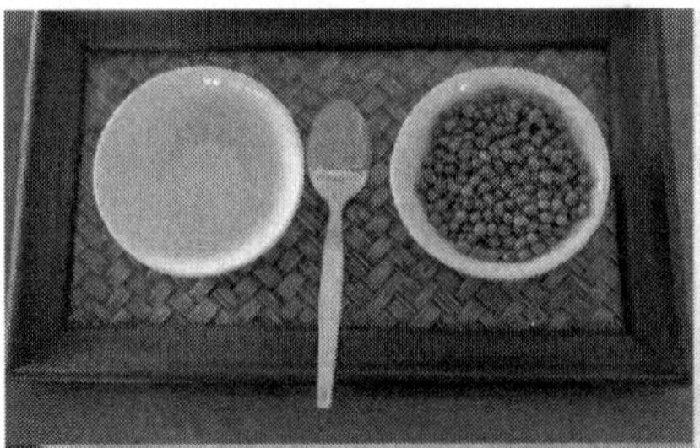
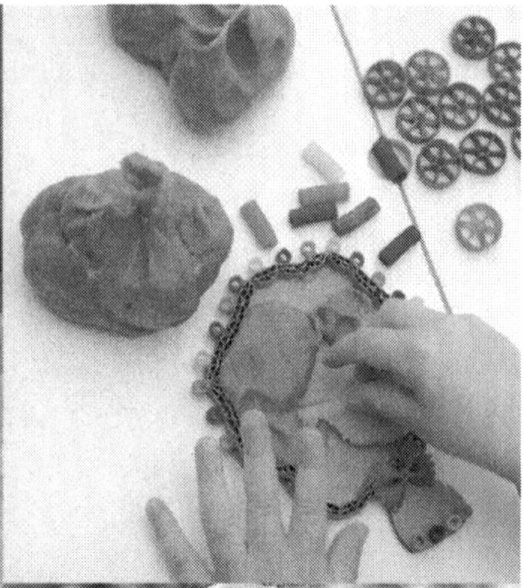
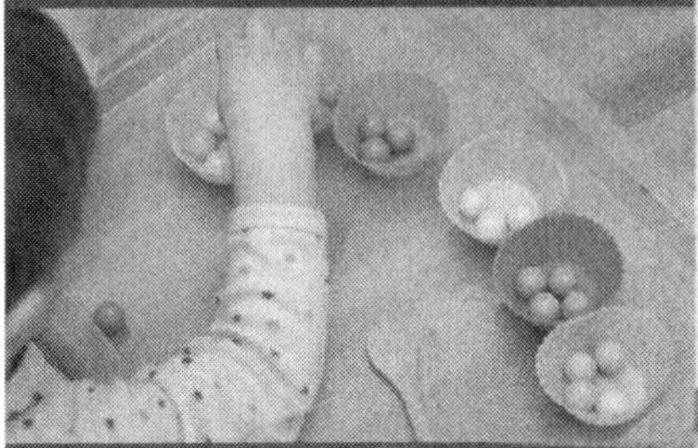
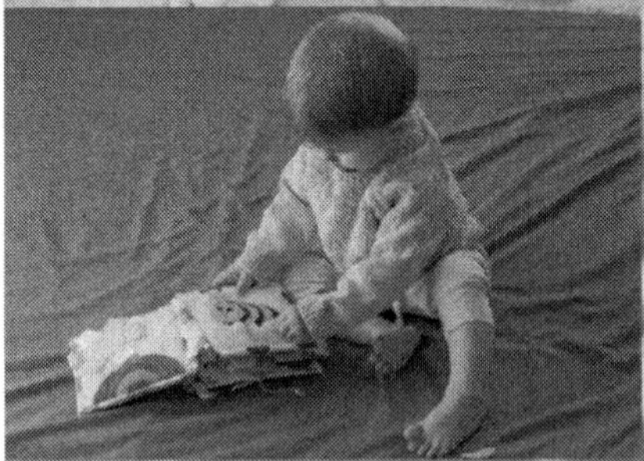
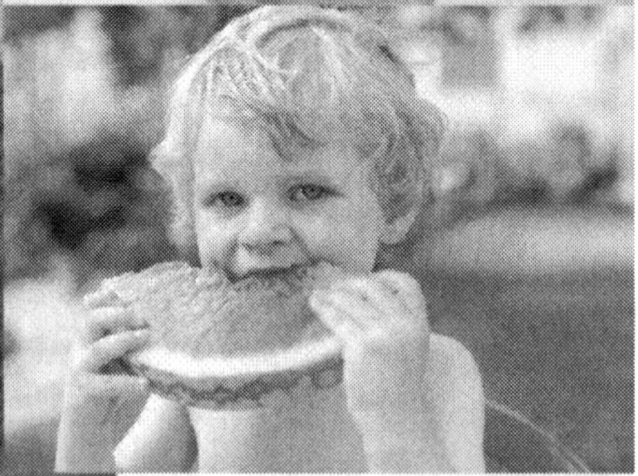
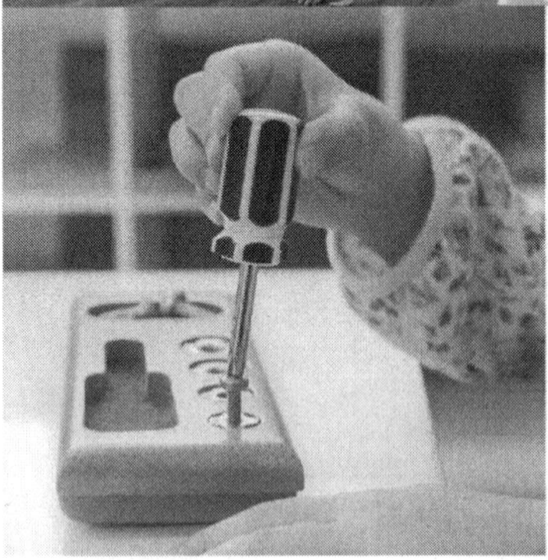
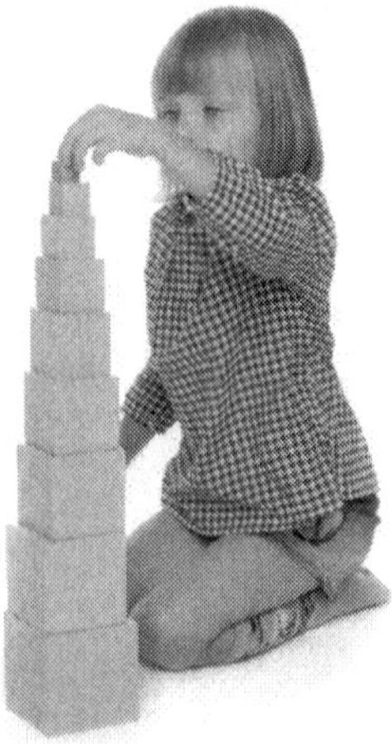

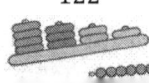

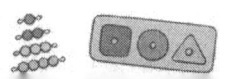

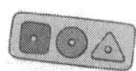

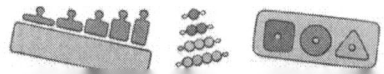

## Development Activities

The developmental activities have multiple purposes but one feature in common: they allow the toddler to develop his mind. To perform these activities, the toddler must have become very familiar with age-appropriate stimulation and sensory and practical life exercises; in this way, he will be able to reach his full potential through developmental exercises that will enable him to:

- Develop visual-motor coordination;
- Improve cognitive skills and logic;
- Perfecting the fine movement of the hand;
- Expand the language
- Develop skills such as concentration and precision and qualities such as patience.

The following are some activities.

*Since 9 Months*

## 91. Painting with Vegetables

Purpose: To train fine hand movement and experiment with color.

Material:

- Large drawing sheet
- 3 small bowls
- Tempera colors (red, yellow, and blue)
- 1 vegetable (potato, zucchini, or carrot)

Place each tempera color in a small bowl and dilute it with a little water. Cut a potato or zucchini in half and show the baby how to pick it up firmly with his hands; dip the vegetable in color and then press it onto the paper. Next, when the baby has performed the movement correctly, have him dip the other half of the vegetable in another primary color and have him print it on the paper. This way, the baby will see how the primary colors combine to create a secondary color.

## 92. Musical Instruments

Purpose: Development of hand fine motor skills and learning different notes.

In addition to introducing your baby to different styles of music, such as classical, jazz, pop, rock, etc., you can introduce him to musical instruments, such as castanets, tambourines, and xylophones. Through these instruments, he develops fine motor skills of the hand, understands that the consequence of his movement corresponds to the production of a sound, and learns to recognize different musical notes. If you offer him a xylophone, ensure that the keys are all of the same material and color so that the little one focuses exclusively on the sound produced by pressing the key. Show him how to use the instruments and leave them at his disposal so he can experience them when he wants to.

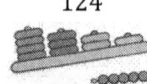

*From 12 Months*

## 93. Drawing with Markers

Purpose: Refinement of fine hand movement and introduction of writing activity.

Material:

- Sheets of paper
- Pen holder
- Large, washable water-based markers, colored pencils, and wax crayons.

Place sheets of paper and a pen holder filled with large, washable water markers on the small table. The toddler will begin to use them to scribble on the paper and see that colored lines are created with every movement he makes. This activity develops his creativity and allows him to see the difference between the thicker lines, the thinner ones, and the dots determined by the pressure of his hand. It also allows him to practice taking off and putting back the cap on the markers. When his fine hand coordination has improved, you can have him experiment with different materials, such as colored pencils and wax crayons.

## 94. Fishing for Small Objects

Purpose: Visual-motor coordination, development of patience, precision, and concentration skills.

Material:

- Tray
- A bowl full of water
- Empty bowl
- Floating objects
- Perforated spoon

- Sponge

Arrange the water-filled bowl on the left side of the tray and the empty one on the right. Place the floating objects in the bowl with water and invite the toddler to transfer them to the empty one using the perforated spoon. This exercise will allow him to develop patience and coordination in his movements, and should he be clumsy and drop water into the tray, he can always undo the damage by using his sponge.

## 95. Construction

Purpose: To introduce solid geometry, and distinguish and divide constructions according to geometric figures.

Constructions allow the toddler to experience the phenomena of statics and balance. Help the toddler learn the names of solids and their physical characteristics and associate them with different colors. For example, you can say, "This cube is yellow," "This cylinder is red," or "The pyramid is taller than the cube"; these terms will stick in his mind, and he will learn the physical differences between different solids, be able to distinguish between them and learn the basics of geometry.

## 96. Lego Duplo

Purpose: To introduce solid geometry, distinguish and divide constructions according to geometric figures, introduce the mathematical concept of fractions, and visual-motor coordination.

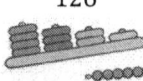

As with building blocks, with Lego Duplo, your toddler develops manual skills and visual-motor coordination. You can use Legos to offer your toddler different activities, such as dividing the pieces by color. On the activity mat, arrange the Legos and two bowls and invite the toddler to divide the pieces by putting each color in the corresponding bowl (you can tell him, for example, which one is red and which is blue). Even if he doesn't distinguish them, by separating the pieces by color, the toddler will immediately notice the mistake when he sees a different color from the others in the bowl.

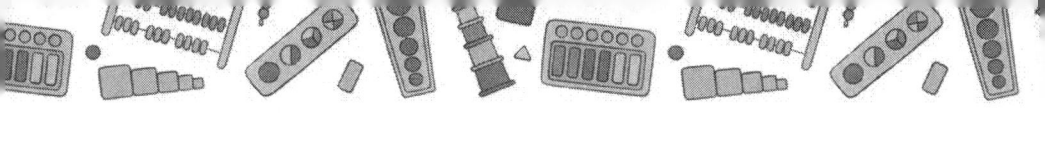

Legos also allow you to learn the basic concepts of fractions. You can, for example, show your toddler the different solid figures, such as the cube or the parallelepiped, and tell him that he is the cube and the exact half of the parallelepiped. You can do this with all solid figures.

## 97. The Tambourine, Rhythm, and Dance

Purpose: To improve cognitive skills, and sharpen coordination and balance.

Listening to music stimulates areas of the brain that improve cognitive abilities, while playing an instrument involves activating areas of the brain related to language use. But that's not all! When toddlers practice playing an instrument, they learn to move following a rhythm; while dancing, they make a considerable effort to achieve balance. You can take advantage of the times when kids show particular interest in music to do small exercises. Along with the dance rhythm, try to maintain balance on one foot, standing on your toes, raising your arms to the sky, lifting first one knee and then the other, and so on. These exercises that may seem very simple have a major impact on the different areas of the brain that allow your toddler to work muscles and mind.

## 98. The Names

Purpose: expansion of language.

When you are with your toddler, help him develop his language as much as possible through knowledge of new terms and especially specific terms. If, for example, you are taking a walk in the garden with him, don't just talk about the different forms of life by saying what kind they are (e.g., plant, tree, bird) but try to be as precise as possible by stating their type; or, when naming body parts, don't just say hand or fingers but tell the toddler what all the fingers and toes are called, and so on. In this way, he will learn new terms and be able to associate the word with the object in question.

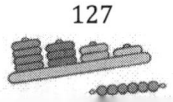

## 99. The Space

Purpose: Expansion of language and perception of space around oneself.

Always try to use terms that enable him to understand how to orient himself in space, e.g., "above and below," "in front and behind," "besides," "near and far," etc. These words allow him to give order to things by determining where they are. To imprint these concepts in his mind, you can play with him by asking him, for example, to put his stuffed animal on top of the bed, under the table, in front of the closet, next to the carpet, and so on. Through play, he will learn the concepts of space and orientation and acquire new terms in his language.

## 100. The Beads

Purpose: Development of visual motor coordination, hand fine motor skills, concentration, and precision.

Material:

- Stick or string
- Colorful pearls

If your toddler cannot hold the string, you can start by presenting him with a stick or wand inside which he can string large beads; when he has become familiar with these activities and is very precise in stringing the beads, you can replace the stick with a string. Show him how to hold the string and string the bead, then let him practice independently without disturbing him so that he does not lose concentration. You will notice that at first, he will put the beads on without caring about color or size; later, when he has mastered the movement, he will be able to choose and alternate between them.

## 101. Matryoshkas

Purpose: To classify and arrange in order of size, development of hand fine motor skills, and concentration skills.

Matryoshkas allow the toddler to observe different sizes, sort objects by size, and arrange them in order. Matryoshkas are very versatile in that they allow not only for arranging boxes in size order but also for building towers, discovering balance, and putting things inside them.

## 102. The Cart

Purpose: Development of motor skills, concentration skills, and autonomy.

Material:

- Wooden box
- Sandpaper
- Felt
- Lanyard

Provide your toddler with a small cart or make a very simple do-it-yourself one. Take a very sturdy wooden fruit crate and smooth it out with sandpaper. Glue felt underneath and in the corners so your little one can easily drag it across the floor without scratching it. Finally, tie a string to the cart so it can be dragged without too much effort.

The toddler can enjoy loading his favorite stuffed animals or toys onto the cart and carrying them around the house. Dragging and pushing are some of the toddlers' favorite activities, allowing them to develop fine motor skills and learn force management.

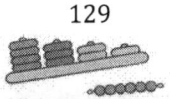

## 103. Activity Panel

Purpose: Development of fine motor skills of the hand.

The activity panel provides a real gym for your toddler. He can practice fine hand movement through the panel by opening and closing locks, latches, and padlocks or turning switches on and off. When he has mastered the use of the objects you have suggested in the activity panel, you can add others, such as wheels, screws, bolts, carabiners, etc.

*For 15 Months*

## 104. Piggy Bank Box

Purpose: To develop hand-eye coordination and pincer grip between the thumb and fingers.

The hole in this box consists of a small slot inside which the toddler must insert the tokens. The learning process is the same as the other boxes. First, the toddler will familiarize himself with the tokens by studying them carefully on his mat; then, he will practice inserting them into the hole by watching how they fall on the mat, and finally, he will open the drawer to pick them up. The difficulty of this exercise lies in the shape of the material: unlike the other materials that were easy to grasp, because they required the opening of the hand, the tokens must be grasped with a thumb and forefinger to be inserted into the hole. This particular shape allows the toddler to develop gripper grasping between the thumb and the other fingers of the hand.

*18 Months:*

## 105. Nomenclature Charts

Purpose: classify objects, observe, expand vocabulary, divide objects into groups by category and quality, and become familiar with writing and reading.

Nomenclature cards have a photograph of an object with its name written in cursive or block letters. You can use nomenclature cards for different activities. Initially, you can divide them into categories and place them in different boxes by offering the toddler one category at a time; have them see one card at a time and names the object represented so they can learn numerous vocabulary words. After presenting all the cards and arranging them on the table, name an object and ask him to find it.

When the toddler is familiar with the vocabulary and object associations, you can increase the difficulty of the exercise by using another deck of identical nomenclature cards. At this point, you can ask him to associate the same figures, and if he makes a mistake, he will notice it himself; or you can ask him to classify the cards according to color; he will put all yellow objects on a yellow card, red objects on the red card, and so on. This way, he will learn to distinguish colors, and if he misclassifies, he will notice. If you have presented the toddler with many nomenclature cards of different categories, you can use the cards to classify objects according to categories. Shuffle them and then ask him to sort them by classifying fruit, animals, transportation, etc.; he will have to look at one card at a time and then place it in the corresponding deck.

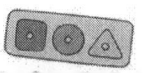

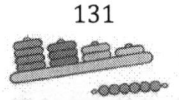

## 106. Memory

Purpose: To develop concentration, language, mnemonic and cognitive skills.

This activity also consists of using nomenclature cards. Begin by using the double decks of cards from one category; arrange all the cards face down and have the toddler turn over two of them. Pass them around until he finds the same ones and can associate them all.

When he has mastered the exercise, you can increase the difficulty by naming the objects on the cards he picks up from time to time; ask him what object it is and let him name it. Then propose that he find the other equal card; in this way, he will quickly learn all the terms associated with the pictures and expand his vocabulary.

You can further increase the difficulty of the exercise by having the toddler take two cards at a time, and if the cards are the same, he will have to put them aside, but if they are different, he will have to turn them face down again. This exercise will enable him to develop strong concentration skills and train his memory so that he will be able to associate the same figures.

## 107. Symmetry

Purpose: To learn the visual concept of symmetry and observation.

Material:

- Sheet of paper
- Temperas
- Brush

Fold a piece of paper in half and let your toddler paint only on one side of the paper. When he finishes his drawing, fold the sheet and let him see what appears on the other side. This activity will allow him to discover the concept of symmetry visually. Provide him with more sheets of paper and let him experience how symmetry generates other shapes.

## 108. The Paper Doll

Purpose: To understand proportions and discover one's own body.

Material:

- Large sheet of paper
- Pencils and colors

On a large sheet of paper, trace the outline of the toddler and cut it out; then, with him, draw in proportion all the elements of the body: the eyes, mouth, hands, clothes, etc. This body outline will make him aware of his body and allow him to study its details and learn new terms.

## 109. Print

Purpose: To train fine hand movement and develop observation and reflection skills.

Material:

- Basket with various leaves of different shapes and sizes (parsley, rosemary, sage, bay leaf, etc.)
- Rough sheets
- Watercolors
- Brushes

Ask your toddler to paint the underside of the leaf with watercolors, then flip it over on the rough paper and press. Ask them: How does the imprint left by the leaf look? Is it uniform? Is it dotted? Why? Ask questions in a way that stimulates his thinking and observation skills, then let him continue to experiment with the print with other leaves. What differences do you notice?

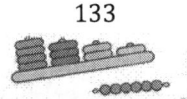

Over time you can increase the difficulty of the exercise by printing the fruit cut in half and introducing the concept of geometry.

## For 2 1/2 Years

### 110. Puzzles

Purpose: To develop logic skills and fine motor skills of the hand.

Choose puzzles depicting nature and show the toddler how to grasp the prehension button with his three fingers and place it in the right place without making a noise. He will practice this action by assembling and disassembling the puzzle until he develops his logic and performs the act with extreme precision.

### 111. Role-playing Games

Purpose: To develop imagination.

Toddlers like to create imaginary worlds in which they experiment with different roles and enjoy impersonating them; for example, they imagine they are parents or pretend to cook. In their minds, they try to reproduce everything they see adults doing and pretend to do the same in their little world made of custom-made objects. When you see your toddler immersed in this activity, do not disturb them or intervene unless they specifically request your presence. Their minds try to process everyday feelings and experiences in these moments by reproducing them in a fantasy world. The most beloved role-playing games are:

- Pretending to be parents;
- Taking care of the dolls as their toddlers;
- Pretending to do the shopping;
- Pretending to cook;
- Pretending to be traders and buyers.

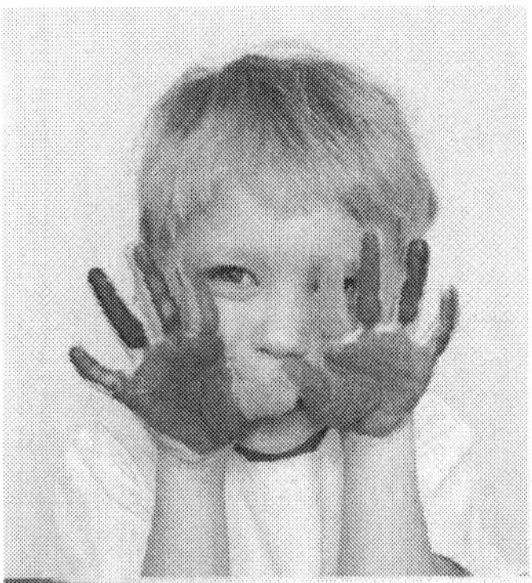
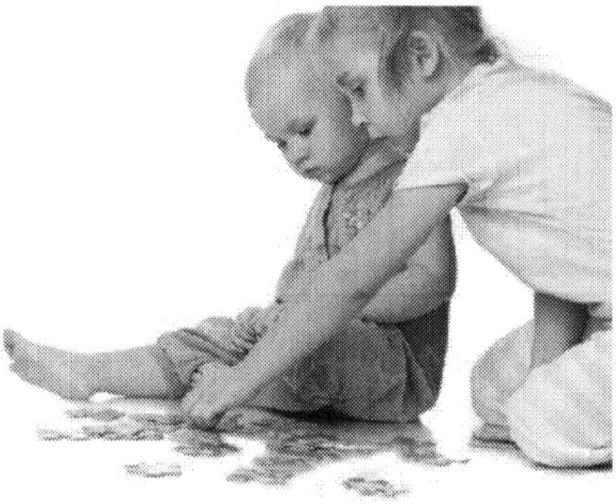
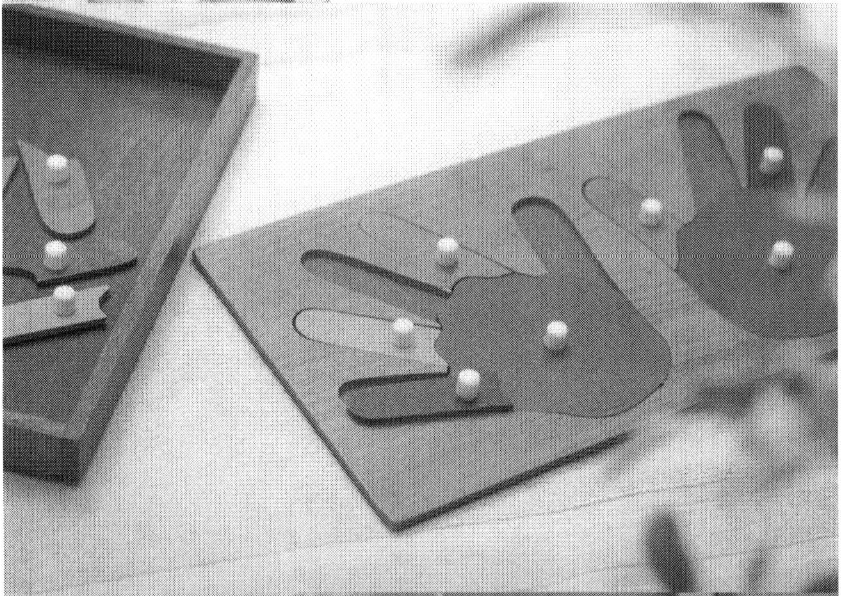
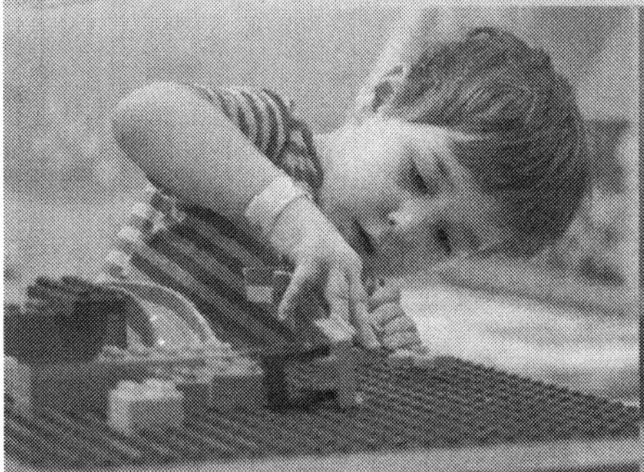
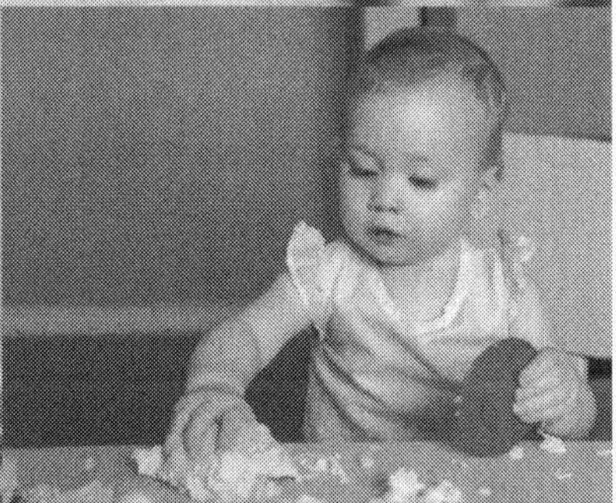

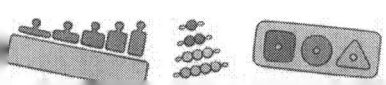

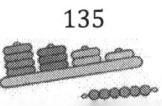

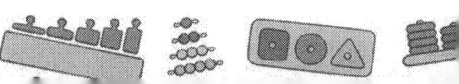

# Chapter 8: Montessori Outdoor Activities

Unfortunately today, it is more and more common to see children attached to smartphones and TVs rather than seeing them playing in the great outdoors. Playing outdoors is very important because it allows the child to grow and develop in the best way possible. Observing nature allows him to hone his sensory skills and also develop a deep interest in every living thing; he sees how trees, flowers, grass, and plants grow and transform and learn to respect and treat them with care. All of this has a strong impact not only at the learning level but also at the cognitive, emotional, and sensory levels.

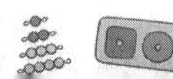

Scientific studies have shown that the benefits of contact with nature include: a general sense of well-being, self-discipline, reduction of depressive disorders and problem behaviors in children, growth in self-esteem, autonomy, and creativity, stimulation of sociability, and development of empathy and civic sense. In particular, a study in Belgium on a sample of 620 children showed that living in a green-rich environment decreased the likelihood of acquiring problem behaviors and strengthened their IQ. [25]

Other research has shown that nature makes it possible to manage disorders such as concentration and attention difficulties and attention deficit hyperactivity disorder. In children living near green areas, it has been noted that the volume of the prefrontal and premotor cortex (the brain regions involved in working memory and attention maintenance mechanisms) is greater.

In addition to having beneficial effects, outdoor activity also has a preventive effect regarding the development of the musculoskeletal system, cardiorespiratory, metabolic, and cancer diseases, and also acts as an anti-stress and anti-anxiety agent.

The benefits of spending time in nature are indeed many. Children have the right to experience nature, and the task of the adult is to help them merge with it by getting to know it, studying its characteristics, and admiring it. Maria Montessori often emphasized the importance of bringing children closer to nature by teaching and cultivating this feeling; in this regard, she expressed herself in the following words:

*"The feeling of nature grows with exercise like anything else, and it is certainly not transfused by us with some description or exhortation made pedantically before an inert and bored child enclosed within walls and accustomed to seeing or hearing that cruelty to animals is a necessity of life. (...) We owe children a reparation rather than a lesson. We must heal the*

---

[25] BIJNENS E.M - DEROM C. - THIERY E. - WEYERS S. - NAWROT T.S., *Residential green space and child intelligence and behavior across urban, suburban, and rural areas in Belgium: A longitudinal birth cohort study of twins, Plos Medicine,* August 18, 2020, in https://journals.plos.org/plosmedicine/article?id=10.1371/journal.pmed.1003213.

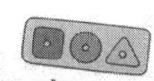

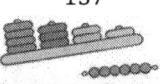

*unconscious wounds, the spiritual illnesses, that are already found in these pretty little children of the prisoners of the artifactual environment."* [26]

Nature is, therefore, a powerful source of experience for the child. There are many ways to encourage contact with nature, such as moving and playing, creating a garden, and caring for an animal. Through movement in the open air, the child can implement everything in their mind, such as running, jumping, climbing, hanging, riding a bike, etc.; in addition, carefully observing everything around them (such as flowers and leaves) allows them to let their imagination and creativity explode by using the materials offered by nature to model something and have new sensory experiences.

Another way a child can be introduced to greenery is to include him in creating a vegetable garden. Taking care of plants allows the child to develop qualities such as patience, a sense of responsibility, and a love of nature; it will also increase their interest and desire to discover how a small seed transforms into a beautiful plant that bears flowers and fruit.

So guide your little one in discovering nature and allow him to experience it! In this section, you will find many useful ideas for air activities to stimulate his mind and motor skills.

---

[26] M. MONTESSORI, *La scoperta del bambino*, Garzanti, Milan, 1999.

*From 12 months*

## 112. Rain

Purpose: To understand the importance of silence, and to discover atmospheric phenomena and their effects on the surrounding environment.

Material:

- Boots
- Waterproof sheet

Rain provides toddlers with a unique sensory experience, bringing them closer to nature and allowing them to discover everything around them through their 5 senses. You can take advantage of a not-too-cold rainy day to take your toddlers on an adventure; after wearing raincoats and booties, invite them to be quiet so that they can hear the sound of the rain; it's ticking more or less loudly; they can smell it, taste it and see how plants, stones, flowers, and trees change color when the rain falls on them.

## 113. Snowmen

Purpose: To stimulate fine hand dexterity, develop creativity and imagination, and increase the sense of freedom and autonomy.

Snow is a very fun event for toddlers. You can take advantage of a snow day or a day in the mountains to introduce your toddler to it, study it, touch it, taste it, and look at it with a magnifying glass. You can make snowmen with him using buckets and shovels if the snowfall is heavy. Don't forget the famous carrot for the snowman's nose and buttons for his eyes. Let him be free to play and experiment, and do not interrupt his concentration.

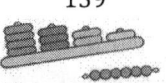

## 114. Listening to the Wind

Purpose: To conquer silence and develop hearing.

The conquest of silence is one of the principles of the Montessori Method. If you get toddlers accustomed to listening by being quiet, they will be able to develop their hearing and discover all the sounds that nature makes, such as the wind rattling the shutters, passing through the doorway, or the leaves on the trees.

You can extend this experience by making rattles that move with the wind. You can use empty jars of different materials, shapes, and sizes, tie them together through a string, and then hang them from a tree branch or near the window. On a windy day, the little one can experience the different sounds the wind makes and admire its power.

## 115. Treasure Hunt

Purpose: To foster autonomy and a desire to discover, acquire new terms and learn the cycle of the seasons.

If it is a beautiful sunny day, you can take the opportunity to go to the park with your toddler. Once you get there, leave around him lots of small treasures that you have collected in advance, such as empty shells, flowers, and leaves. Let him study their characteristics and tell him what they are called so that he can associate the name with the object. When he is older, he can search for small treasures on his own (e.g., looking for squirrels, butterflies, flowers, hill ants, etc.) and experience the joy derived from his small-big discoveries. Let him be free to discover without interrupting his moments of concentration, but still, pay attention that he does not pick up dirty objects or objects that might hurt him.

If you regularly take your toddler out into nature, you will allow him to observe everything around him and also how everything changes as the seasons change.

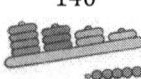

## 116. Treasure Hunt on the Beach

Purpose: To foster autonomy and the desire to discover, and acquire new terms.

If you live near the sea or are on vacation near it, you can take this opportunity to propose a beach treasure hunt for your toddler. In this new environment, he will be able to unleash his curiosity by searching for special nature elements such as shells, sponges, stones with strange shapes and colors, etc. You can then hide his little treasure under the sand and ask him to play at finding it; this way, he will have to dig with his hands and test his mind to orient himself in space.

You can increase the difficulty of the exercise by hiding different treasures under the sand in different places. If other toddlers are present, they can all have fun looking for them together.

*From 18 Months*

## 117. Necklaces

Purpose: To develop concentration skills, patience, and fine motor skills of the hand.

Spring and summer offer many opportunities to see many kinds of flowers popping up; you can take the opportunity to entice your toddlers to pick as many as they can while leaving the stems very long. When they have finished picking them, with much patience and delicacy, they should make a small hole in the stalk of the first flower, inside which they will thread the stem of the second one and so on or pass them through a string. With this method, they can make beautiful flower necklaces, garlands, bracelets, etc. The toddler can also learn a lot from the process of drying the flowers and using them at a later time for decoupage work.

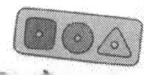

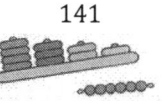

## 118. Shell Necklaces

Purpose: To develop concentration skills, patience, and fine motor skills of the hand.

If you are at the seaside and have already come across treasure hunting with your toddler, it is time to create necklaces with his sea treasures. If there are some among the shells with little holes or slits, you can suggest that he pass a string through them and create a beautiful necklace. He can then have fun decorating the shells with tempera colors and thus create colorful shell necklaces.

## From 2 Years

## 119. The Kite

Purpose: To stimulate orientation, strengthen muscles and the immune system, and increase concentration and self-esteem.

Material:

- Plastic bag or tissue paper
- 4 sticks or plastic straws
- Tape
- Scissors
- Twine
- Cork
- Ribbons or leaves

During windy days you can let your toddler discover the experience of flying a kite in the sky. You can make this moment even more fun if you build it with him. To make it, you need to arrange the little cross-shaped sticks on the plastic sheet and fasten them with tape in the middle and at the ends. Then cut out the bag to form a rhombus, then tie the string in the center. Your toddler may enjoy further embellishing his kite by adding a tail made of ribbons or leaves; at the other end of the twine, tie a cork so that the little one can hold the kite firmly. You are ready to experiment with how high the kite can fly and from which direction the wind is coming.

## 120. The Vegetable Garden

Purpose: To learn how to care for nature and learn about its life cycle.

If you do not have a garden, you can take advantage of any small space to create a small vegetable garden, such as a small yard corner or terrace.

Material:

- Wooden boxes, planters, or jars
- Soil
- Watering can
- Sprayer

In winter, put potting soil inside wooden boxes, planters, or jars; when spring comes, depending on the space you have available, you can sow herbs, vegetables, or fruits together with your toddler.

Watch his reaction when small seedlings begin to sprout from the seeds. Teach him to take care of them by watering them from time to time with his little watering can and, when they have grown, to spray the leaves with the sprayer. Making a vegetable garden is a great time of growth for your toddler's mind, who learns not only the cycle of nature through his experience but also how to care for other forms of life. When the plants have grown, and it is time to harvest their fruits, you can offer many other activities, such as sensory activities to learn to recognize the different scents of herbs or to learn to recognize tastes and associate them with each fruit or vegetable.

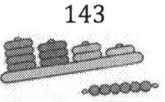

## 121. The Masks

Purpose: To discover the cycle of nature and develop hand fine motor skills.

Material:

- Leaves of different types and colors
- Scissors
- Glue

If your toddler has become familiar with decoupage, you can suggest that he make masks by collecting different leaves of different colors. This way, he will have fun looking for leaves in the garden, see how they change color according to the season, and discover the differences between one leaf and another. In addition, using scissors to cut out and glue to glue will allow him to develop fine hand motor skills..

## 122. Playing With Puddles

Purpose: To stimulate motor skills and the 5 senses, encourage contact with nature and increase self-esteem and autonomy.

Arm your toddler with a raincoat, rubber boots, and old pants, and let him discover the amazing world created by rain and puddles. He can have fun jumping in it by lifting as much water as he can or long-wing without falling in; he can watch how wooden sticks and leaves float in it or admire its reflection. Even if you have to wash all your clothes afterward, don't deprive your toddlers of having this wonderful experience that nature gives during the changing seasons.

## 123. Skittles

Purpose: To develop motor skills, knowledge of the body and one's limits, improve balance and increase self-esteem.

Material:

- Empty, colored plastic bottles or colored cardboard rolls
- 1 ball

Even before leaving home, the toddler can enjoy decorating empty plastic bottles or cardboard rolls, and then, once you reach the park, he can play with his friends with skittles. Have the toddler place the pins a few feet away from him and not too close to each other; then, ask him to take turns throwing the ball and knocking down as many pins as possible. This exercise will help him measure his strength, increase his balance, and also his self-esteem. If this game becomes too easy, you can increase its difficulty by adding water inside the bottles; this way, the toddler will have to exert much more force to knock them down.

## 124. The Tire

Purpose: To develop motor skills, knowledge of the body and one's limits, improve balance and increase self-esteem.

The tire is a very versatile tool indeed for toddlers to play with. You can place it on a lawn or hang it with a rope from a strong tree branch. Toddlers will have a lot of fun jumping in and out of the tire or using it as a swing; this activity will stimulate movement and balance.

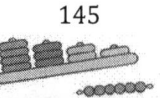

## 125. Planting a Tree

Purpose: To foster contact with nature, observe its changes and growth process, and increase a sense of responsibility.

Material:

- Tree
- Spade
- Barrel
- Rope
- Watering can

Allowing toddlers to plant a tree in the garden at home, school, or the country is a very enriching experience. With a spade, make a hole in the earth and insert the roots inside it, paying attention to picking them up well; cover it and have the toddler jump on the earth. Explain to him that it is important to help the tree and support it, and to do this, you will use a cane to put next to the trunk and a rope with which to tie it. Have the toddler water the ground and then give him the task of coming back once a week to give it some water. It will create a sense of responsibility, interest, and protection towards the nature around him, and he will be able to observe its changes over time.

## 126. The Bird Feeder

Purpose: To encourage contact with nature and increase a sense of responsibility.

Material:

- Empty yogurt pots
- Bowl
- Twine
- Scissors
- Lard
- Seeds: sunflower, wheat, oat, millet, etc.
- Chopped dried fruits: walnuts, chopped hazelnuts, raisins, etc.

Take some well-cleaned yogurt jars with your toddler and make a hole in the bottom. Take a string, cut a piece long enough, and thread it through the hole in the jar, making a big knot from the inside. Let the lard soften at room temperature, then put it inside the bowl and add all the other ingredients. Have your toddler mix the mixture with his hands, and then, with the help of a spoon, have him pour it into the jars. Let the jars sit in the refrigerator for a few hours, after which they will be ready to be hung on the branches upside down. At this point, all the little one has to do is watch the birds approach, see how they eat and listen to the sounds they make.

## 127. Sandcastles

Purpose: To unleash creativity and imagination, encourage contact with nature, and stimulate touch.

One way toddlers can unleash their imaginations at the seaside is to create sand castles or sculptures. Let them be free to make, get dirty, and imagine. As their hands work, so makes their mind, so don't distract them and let them be immersed in their stimulating and fun activity.

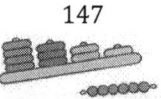

## 128. Soap Bubbles

Purpose: To unleash creativity and develop motor coordination.

The magic of soap bubbles has always fascinated toddlers (and adults, too!). You can make magical soap bubbles with your little one on a beautiful sunny day. The sunlight, reflecting the rainbow colors, will provide a fantastic visual experience.

Material:

- A straw
- One meter of twine
- Basin with water and liquid soap

Cut the straw in half and thread each piece onto one end of the string. Dip the string into the bowl of liquid soap and advise your toddler not to let go. At this point sway the string until a giant soap bubble appears! Let your toddler repeat the experience on his own for as long as he wishes.

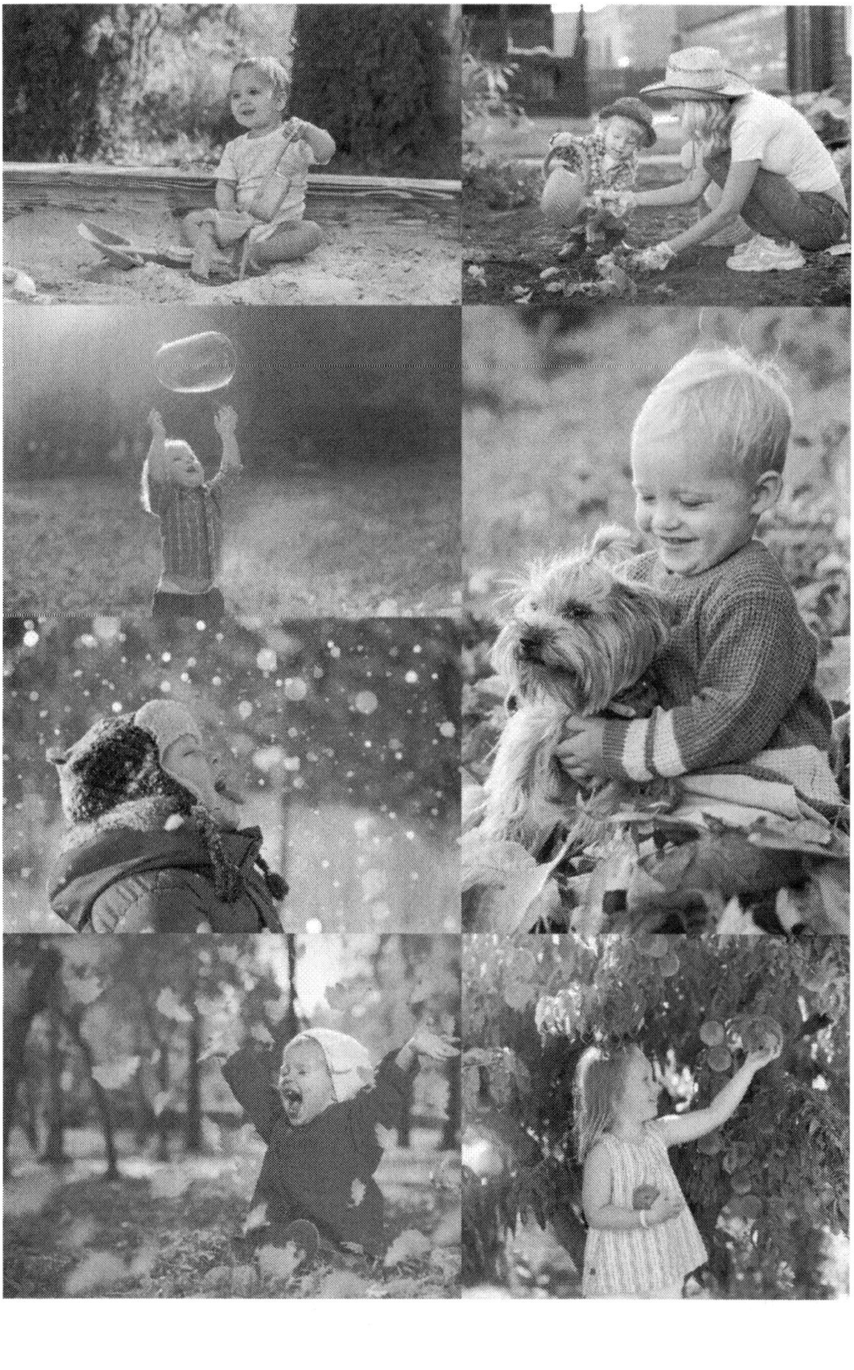

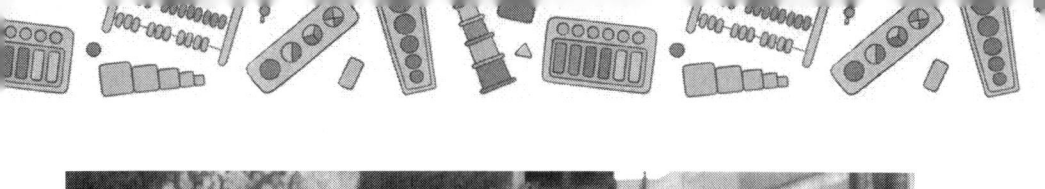

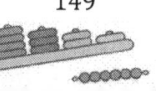

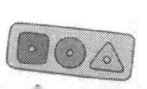

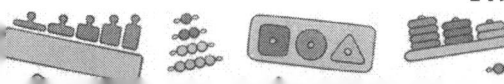

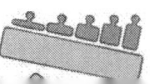

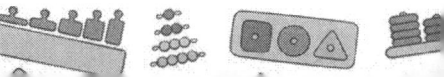

# Chapter 9: Recipes for the Youngest

In Chapter 8, we have provided many hints of practical life activities that you can offer toddlers to introduce them to the kitchen and to gain self-confidence, self-esteem, and independence. But why is it so important to invite your toddler to cooperate in the activities that take place in the kitchen?

## *Reasons to Involve Your Toddler in the Kitchen*

There are indeed many reasons to involve a toddler in activities carried out in the kitchen, but we will mention 10:

1. Certainly, the first is to make the most of his **absorbent mind**, that is, the ability to learn spontaneously and very quickly from all the stimuli that are provided by his surroundings;
2. A second reason is to allow him to use his hands to experiment and discover, thus fulfilling one of his main needs and, at the same time, allowing him to develop hand muscles and visual-motor coordination;

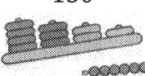

3. Allow them to develop the 5 senses by having constructive experiences;
4. Allow him to practice repetition of an activity until he masters it completely and develops strong concentration skills;
5. Enrich vocabulary by learning new terms;
6. Applying mathematics to reality;
7. Help him become autonomous and develop executive functions (working memory, inhibitory control, and cognitive flexibility);
8. Stimulate the senses and refine the palate;
9. Help him learn about foods and nature;
10. To transmit values to him.

In this chapter, we will propose recipes your toddler can learn to make independently (always under your supervision but without interfering). First, it is important to provide him with the right tools to "do it himself." Let's look at some of them.

## Tools

In Chapter 6, we looked at how to organize a Montessori-style kitchen. Now we will do a brief roundup of the tools you can provide for your little one so that he can make recipes on his own but safely. These are:

- Learning tower;
- Tailored apron;
- Suitable tools:
    - Easy-to-carry cutting board;
    - Carafe with medium-sized spout;
    - Wooden spoon;
    - Butter knife and paring knife;
    - Rolling pin and whisk;
    - Potato peeler, a grater with a non-slip handle, and a potato masher.

Also, remember to reserve a cupboard in the lower part of the kitchen so that he can keep his accessories in order: his small bowls, his mops, his utensils, and even the ingredients to make his snack.

Now you are ready to make the recipes we are about to propose together with your toddler; then, once the little one has learned the perfect execution of the movements and their succession, you can let him do it himself!

Also in this section, we have divided the recipes according to the age group to keep up with the toddler's progress. Always remember not to force him to do a particular activity; if it is too difficult, postpone it to another time. Follow his progress and let him choose.

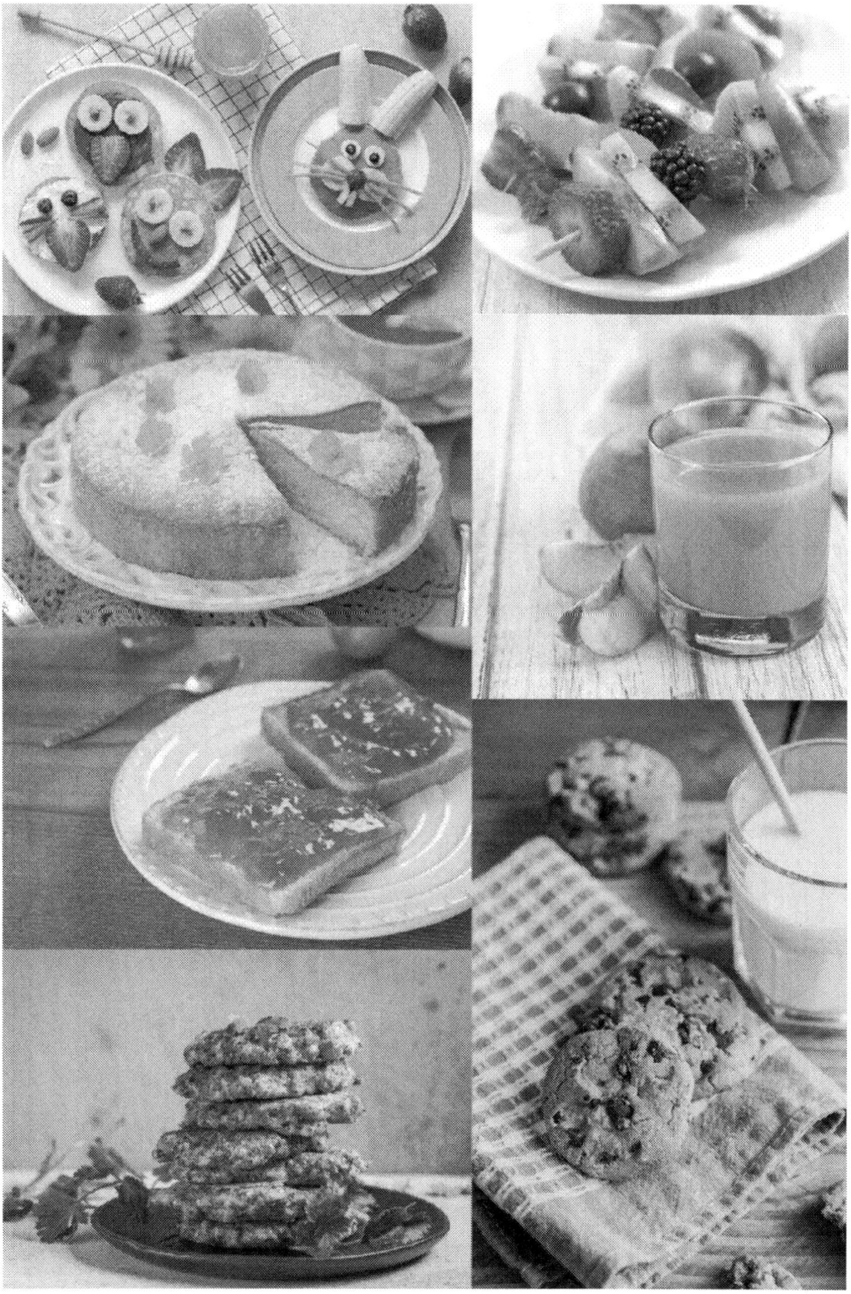

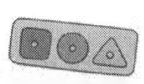

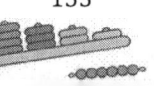

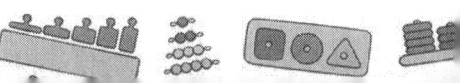

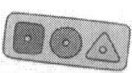

## From 2 Years

### 1. Fans with Jam

*Preparation: 40 min | Cooking: 15 min | Servings: 10*
*Ingredients:*

- 1 roll of puff pastry
- 1/3 jar of jam of your choice

*Directions:*

1. Line a baking sheet with parchment paper and set aside.
2. Gently unroll the puff pastry on the surface, then spread the jam on top. Roll one side of the pastry up to the center, then do the same with the other side. Place in the freezer for 30 minutes. Meanwhile, preheat the oven to 400°F.
3. Cut the roll into slices about 1 cm thick and place them on the baking paper. Bake for 12 minutes, then set to grill mode and bake another 3 minutes until golden brown. Let cool completely, then transfer the fans to an airtight container.

*What the toddler can do:* they can unroll the puff pastry, roll and cut it, spread the jam, arrange fans on the baking paper, check the baking, and transfer the fans to the container.

## 2.  Cream milk and cookies

*Preparation: 10 min | Cooking: 5 min | Servings: 2*
*Ingredients:*

- 1 ¼ cup whole milk
- 30 Plasmon-type cookies
- 1 tablespoon of honey

*Directions:*

1. Place the milk and honey in a small saucepan and heat over medium heat, stirring until the honey is dissolved. Add the crumbled cookies and stir well until completely dissolved. Cook for a few minutes until thickened. Remove the saucepan from the heat, let the cream cool, and pour it into the cups sprinkling with some crumbled Plasmon.

*What the toddler can do:* crumble the cookies and weigh the ingredients.

## 3.  Milk-shake

*Preparation: 5 min. | Servings: 4*
*Ingredients:*

- 2 cup milk
- 1 cup frozen milk or vanilla ice cream
- 1 cup fresh raspberries
- 1 tablespoon of jam

*Directions:*

1. Wash the raspberries well and place them in the freezer for about 1 hour.
2. In a blender, place the milk, ice cream, frozen raspberries, and jam and blend for a few minutes until smooth. Pour the milkshake into glasses, garnish with fresh raspberries, and enjoy.

*What the toddler can do:* crumble the cookies and weigh the ingredients.

## 4. Jam

*Preparation: 20 min. | Cooking: 30 min. | Servings: 2 jars*

Ingredients:

- 4 lbs. of apricots or your favorite fruit
- 2 cups of sugar
- Juice of 1 lemon

Directions:

1. Choose ripe and unblemished fruit, wash them well, and dry them on a tea towel; cut the apricots in half, remove the stone, cut them into wedges, and transfer them to a bowl. Then, add the sugar, squeeze the juice from the lemon, strain it through a fine-mesh strainer, add the juice to the bowl, and stir with a ladle. Cover with the bowl lid or plastic wrap and let macerate in the refrigerator overnight.
2. Pour everything into a pot and bring it to a boil. Cook for 30 minutes, stirring occasionally. Once ready, decant the jam into sanitized jars and screw on the caps.

*What the toddler can do:* he can wash the fruit, dry it, cut it into pieces, and decant it into the bowl; he can decant the sugar, squeeze the lemon, strain the juice, and pour it into the bowl; he can stir it with the ladle and screw the caps on.

## 5. Smoothie

Smoothies are milk-based smoothies that the child can make with the fruit of the child's choice. The following are of different colors so the child can have fun sorting the fruit by color. The process is the same for all.

*Preparation: 1 hour. 5 min. | Portions: 1 cup*
*Ingredients*

*Yellow:*

- ½ cup of mangoes or peaches
- 1 passion fruit or ½ cup apricots
- ½ banana
- ½ cup of water
- ½ cup of coconut milk or whole milk

*Pink:*

- 5 strawberries
- 1 raspberry
- ½ cup dehydrated coconut
- ½ cup of milk

*Violet:*

- ½ cup of blueberries
- ½ cup of strawberries
- ½ cup of red grapes
- ½ cup of soy or rice milk

*Green:*

- 2 cups of spinach
- ½ cup avocado
- ¼ cup of pineapple
- 1 cup of apple juice
- ½ cup of milk

*Directions:*

1. Clean and cut the fruit you have chosen into pieces. Transfer it inside freezer-friendly bags, then place them in the freezer overnight. Pour the contents of the bag into the blender and add the drink. Blend for about 1 minute, then transfer to a glass.

*What the toddler can do:* wash and cut fruits and vegetables and distribute them in the different bags according to color; dose the ingredients.

## 6. Chocolate Filled Cookies

*Preparation: 15 min | Cooking: 10 min | Servings: 12*
*Ingredients:*

- 2½ oz sugar or 3 tablespoons honey
- 1/3 cup of coconut oil
- ¼ cup soy, oat, or rice milk
- 1 ¼ cup flour (OO, oat, rice, or whole wheat)
- 6 chocolate squares cut in half
- 1 pinch of salt

*Directions:*

1. Preheat the oven to 350°F and line a baking sheet with baking paper.
2. In a medium-sized bowl, mix the coconut oil and sugar until smooth. Slowly add the milk, stirring continuously. Finally, combine the flour and salt and knead with your hands until you get a ball.
3. Divide the dough into 12 portions and create balls. Flatten the balls with the palm of your hand, place half a square of chocolate on each disk, and fold the dough tightly over the chocolate, closing the edges carefully.
4. Bake for 10 minutes and let cool for 5 minutes before enjoying.

*What the toddler can do:* he can dose the ingredients, mix the oil and sugar, knead, shape the balls, and arrange the cookies on the baking sheet.

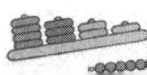

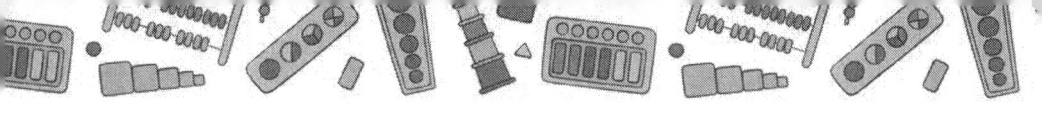

## 7. Chocolate Chip Cookies

*Preparation: 15 min | Cooking: 10 min | Servings: 12*
*Ingredients:*

- 1/3 cup coconut or olive oil
- ½ cup of brown sugar
- ¼ cup granulated sugar
- ¼ cup of milk
- 1 teaspoon of cornstarch
- 1 teaspoon vanillin
- 1 ½ cups of flour
- 1 pinch of salt
- 1 pinch of baking soda
- ½ cup of chocolate chips

*Directions:*

1. Preheat the oven to 350°F and line a baking sheet with baking paper.
2. In a bowl, mix the oil and sugar; add the milk, starch, and vanillin and mix well; incorporate the flour, baking soda, and salt. Finally, add the chocolate chips and knead them by hand.
3. Using an ice cream scoop, scoop out the dough and place 12 balls on baking paper. Bake for 10 minutes and let cool for 5 minutes before enjoying.

*What the toddler can do:* dose the ingredients, decant, mix, knead, and arrange the cookies on the baking sheet.

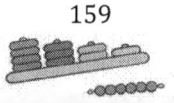

## 8. Almond Milk

*Preparation: 10 min. + 1 night | Servings: 3 glasses*
Ingredients:

- 4 oz almonds or hazelnuts
- 1/3 cup. of water
- 1 tablespoon of honey (optional)

Directions:

1. Pour the dried fruit into a bowl, add water, and let it soak overnight. Take it out with a strainer, rinse it with plenty of water, and keep the soaking water aside. Transfer the dried fruit to a blender and, after straining, add the soaking water. If you wish, add a tbsp of honey before blending at maximum power for 1 minute.
2. Place a towel over a bowl and pour the liquid into it. Strain all the liquid by pressing the cloth well, then pour it into a bottle and store it in the refrigerator for up to 5 days.

*What the toddler can do:* dose and mix the ingredients, and press the smoothie to extract the strained liquid.

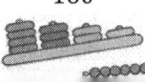

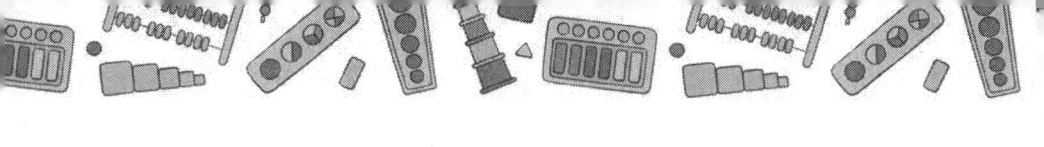

## 9. Yogurt

*Preparation: 10 min. + 16 hrs. | Cooking: 5 min. | Servings: 6*

*Ingredients:*

- 4 cups of whole milk
- ½ cup Greek yogurt or one sachet of lactic acid bacteria

*Procedure:*

1. Pour the milk into a saucepan and heat it to a temperature of 110°F. Meanwhile, pour the Greek yogurt into a bowl, and as soon as the milk has reached temperature, pour a cup of it into the yogurt. With a whisk, stir well until the lumps are dissolved, then pour the mixture into the pot with the milk and stir.
2. Transfer to a jar with a lid or to a large bowl covered with foil. Cover the jar or bowl with a tea towel and secure it with a rubber band. Cover further with a woolen blanket and let it rest in an oven with a temperature of 77 to 95°F for about 12 hours. After the 12 hours have passed, transfer the yogurt to the refrigerator and let it cool for at least 4 hours before uncovering and serving.

*What the toddler can do:* mix milk and yogurt.

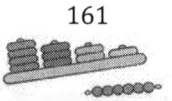

## 10. Scones

Preparation: 30 min. + 2 hours | Cooking: 25 min. | Servings: 9

Ingredients:

- ½ cup lukewarm water
- ½ cup lukewarm milk
- 1 teaspoon dehydrated brewer's yeast
- 1 teaspoon sugar
- ½ tablespoon salt
- 4 tablespoons extra virgin olive oil
- 1 ¼ cup of Manitoba flour
- 1 ¼ cup 00 flour

Directions:

1. In a bowl, mix all flours, baking powder, and sugar.
2. In another bowl, pour the water, oil, milk, and salt and mix. Add the flour mixture a little at a time and mix with a fork. When the dough gains consistency, transfer it to the floured work surface and continue kneading with your hands, adding flour if necessary. Work energetically until the dough is smooth, homogeneous, and elastic. Form it into a ball, cover it with plastic wrap and a tea towel, and let it rest for about 40 minutes. Meanwhile, line a baking sheet with baking paper.
3. Using a rolling pin, roll out the dough to a thickness of half an inch. Using a 5-inch diameter pastry cutter (or a glass or cup), form 9 disks. Place the dough discs on the baking sheet, cover them with foil, and let them rise for about 1 1/2 hours.
4. Preheat oven to 375°F in static mode. After the rising time has elapsed, remove the foil and press on the disks with your fingers, forming 5-6 dimples. Sprinkle with fine salt and bake the scones in the oven for 20-25 minutes. Take the scones out of the oven and, while still warm, wet the surface with water using a small brush.

*What the toddler can do:* dose and mix flours, decant liquids, knead, make discs and dimples, and brush.

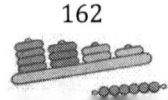

## 11. Milk Sandwiches

*Preparation: 20 min. + 2 hr. 40 min. | Cooking: 15 min. | Portions: 30*

*Ingredients:*

- 3 1/3 cups Manitoba flour
- 1 ½ cup whole milk
- 2 oz butter
- 2 oz sugar
- 1 teaspoon fresh brewer's yeast (or 3g dry brewer's yeast)
- ½ oz salt
- 1 yolk.

*Directions:*

1. Warm the milk slightly to 99°F and dissolve the sugar and crumbled brewer's yeast in it, stirring with a teaspoon.
2. Melt the butter and let it cool.
3. Place all the Manitoba flour in a bowl and make a hole in the center. Gradually add all the milk mixture and turn with a fork. Add the melted butter and salt and continue turning with a fork. When the dough gains consistency, transfer it to the floured work surface and continue kneading with your hands until the dough is smooth. Cover the bowl with plastic wrap and cotton cloth and let the dough rest for about 2 hours until doubled in volume.
4. Line a baking sheet with parchment paper. After the rising time has elapsed, divide the dough into 30 parts, create balls, and place them on the baking sheet. Cover the balls with a clean tea towel and let rise for another 40 minutes.
5. Preheat the oven to 350°F. Brush all the milk buns with beaten egg yolk and bake them for 15 minutes. Let them cool completely before cutting them in half and stuffing them.

*What the toddler can do:* dose the ingredients and mix them, knead, create the balls, separate the yolk from the egg white, and brush the rolls.

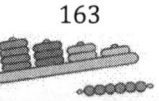

## 12. Orchard

*Preparation: 5 min. + 15 min. | Portions: 3*

*Ingredients:*

- 2½ oz fresh, low-fat yogurt
- 4½ oz fresh spreadable cheese
- 3 teaspoons of honey
- 1 banana
- 3 apricots
- 6 strawberries

*Directions:*

1. Puree the fruits separately with the blender and put them in three different bowls. Add ¾ oz yogurt, 1½ oz spreadable cheese, and 1 teaspoon honey to each bowl. Blend the contents of each bowl, then place the bowls in the refrigerator for at least 15 minutes before enjoying.

*What the toddler can do:* clean and cut fruit, dose yogurt and cheese.

*From 3 Years*

## 13. Pancakes

Preparation: 5 min | Cooking: 50 min | Portions: 10

Ingredients:

- 1 cup vegetable drink
- 2 tablespoons of yeast
- 1 tablespoon of lemon juice
- 5 oz of spelt flour
- 1 tablespoon of cornstarch
- 1 pinch of salt
- 2 tablespoons of maple syrup

Directions:

1. Pour the vegetable drink, lemon juice, and yeast into a bowl. Stir and let stand for 10 min.
2. In another bowl, combine the flour, starch, and salt. Add the liquid mixture and maple syrup and mix.
3. Heat the pan and lightly grease it, then pour in 2 tbsp of batter and cook for about 2 minutes. When bubbles begin to form, flip the pancake and cook on the other side for another 2 minutes. Serve immediately, accompanied with maple syrup, fresh fruit, spread, or compote.

*What the toddler can do:* dose and mix the ingredients, stuff the pancakes, and spread the cream.

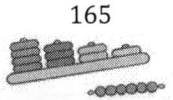

## 14. Pangoccioli (Bread with Chocolate)

Preparation: 15 min. + 2 hours and 30 minutes | Cooking: 25 min. | Portions: 25

Ingredients:

- ½ cup lukewarm water
- ½ oz brewer's yeast
- 1 tablespoon honey
- 4 cup flour
- ½ cup lukewarm milk
- ¼ cup sunflower seed oil
- ½ cup sugar
- 1 egg
- 1 sachet vanillin
- 4 oz dark chocolate chips

Directions:

1. Pour the warm water into a bowl and crumble in the brewer's yeast. Add the tablespoon of honey and 4 oz of flour and mix well. Let stand for 15 minutes.
2. After the resting time has elapsed, add the warm milk, sunflower oil, sugar, egg, and 1 sachet of vanillin and mix well. After that, add all the remaining flour a little at a time, and finally, the dark chocolate chips. Bring the dough to the work surface and knead with your hands until smooth and homogeneous.
3. Transfer the dough to a bowl and carve a cross; cover with plastic wrap and a tea towel and let rise for 2 hours until doubled in volume.
4. Line two baking sheets with baking paper and preheat the oven to 350°F. After the rising time has elapsed, take the dough and knead it with your hands for a few minutes. Divide the dough into 25 portions and form it into balls. Arrange the "pangoccioli" on the baking sheet spaced out, cover them with foil and let them rise for another 30 minutes. Bake in a static oven for 25 minutes.

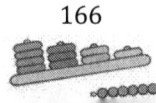

5. Break off small pieces of the dough and form them into balls to place on baking sheets (not too close together because they will grow in the oven). Cover with foil and let rise for another 30 minutes. Bake for 25 minutes and let cool before enjoying.

*What the toddler can do:* weigh and mix ingredients, knead, and form balls.

## 15. Fresh Fruit Skewers

*Preparation: 5 min. | Servings: 6*
*Ingredients:*

- ½ watermelon
- 1 melon
- Grapes, raspberries, blackberries, strawberries, to taste

*Directions:*

1. Wash the fresh fruit and cut it into cubes. Cut the melon in half and remove the seeds. Using a digger, scoop out the melon and watermelon balls and transfer them into small cups. Prepare the skewers by combining the colors of the fruit.

*What the toddler can do:* wash and cut the fruit, empty the melon, and prepare the skewers.

## 16. Cereal bars

*Preparation: 15 min. | Servings: 9*
*Ingredients:*

- 1 cup of oatmeal
- 1 ½ cups of puffed quinoa
- 2 tablespoons of chia seeds
- 1/3 cup coconut flakes
- 1 pinch of salt
- ¼ cup chopped hazelnuts
- ½ cup soft dates pitted and cut into pieces
- 1/3 cup cashew or almond butter
- ¼ cup of honey
- 2 tablespoons of coconut oil
- 1 tablespoon of vanilla extract
- 5 tablespoons of water
- 2 bars of dark chocolate

*Directions:*

1. Add the first 7 ingredients to a bowl and mix.
2. In a saucepan, heat the cashew butter, add sugar, vanilla extract, and water, and mix well. When the mixture is smooth, pour it into the bowl and mix well.
3. Line a 15x20cm baking pan with baking paper and pour the mixture evenly. Place the baking sheet in the freezer for 15 minutes, then take it out and cut 9 bars. Place the baking sheet in the refrigerator for 1 hour.
4. Melt the dark chocolate in a double boiler, then dip one side of the bar into the chocolate. Turn the bar upside down and place it on a baking sheet or tray. Let stand in the refrigerator for 15 minutes before enjoying.

*What the toddler can do:* dose and mix the ingredients, and distribute the mixture in the pan.

## 17. Peach Fruit Juice

Preparation: 15 min | Cooking: 25 min | Portions: 2 L

Ingredients:

- 2 lb 4 oz ripe peaches
- 1 1/3 cup sugar
- 1 US quart of water
- 1 lemon juice

Directions:

1. Choose ripe peaches, wash them, peel them, cut them into pieces, and set them aside in a bowl.
2. In a large pot, pour the water and sugar and cook over medium heat until the sugar is completely dissolved. Add the chopped peaches and cook for 3 minutes from the boiling time. Add the lemon juice and, when finished cooking, remove from the heat and blend with a blender until completely liquid.
3. We bottle the boiling juice into clean, dried glass bottles. Seal with new capsules and allow to cool completely before placing in the refrigerator. Consume the juice within one week.

*What the toddler can do:* weigh and mix the ingredients, wash, and cut the peaches.

## 18. Potato Dumplings

*Preparation: 30 min | Cooking: 30 min | Servings: 4*
*Ingredients:*

- 1 lb 5 oz floury potatoes
- 1 cup flour
- 1 yolk
- salt and pepper to taste

*Directions:*

1. Peel the potatoes and steam them for 25-30 minutes. Once cooked, mash them with a potato masher. Add half the flour, a pinch of salt, and pepper and mix with a fork. Gradually add the remaining flour and egg yolk and knead until you have a soft ball.
2. On floured work surface, divide the dough into 4 portions and shape by forming long cylinders 2 cm thick. Cut the cylinders into 2 cm pieces and press them on the tines of a fork.
3. Bring a pot with plenty of salted water to a boil and pour in the gnocchi. When they come to the surface, remove them with a slotted spoon and season them with the sauce of your choice.

*What the toddler can do:* peel the potatoes, mash them with a potato masher, dose and mix the ingredients, separate the egg white from the yolk, knead, cut the dough, and shape the dumplings with a fork.

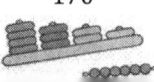

## 19. Creamy Polenta

*Preparation: 5 min | Cooking: 10 min | Servings: 4*

*Ingredients:*

- 1 ¼ cup precooked polenta
- 2 cups. of water
- 1 cup. of milk
- ½ stock cube (vegetable or chicken)
- ½ cup of grated cheese
- Salt and pepper to taste

*Directions:*

1. In a saucepan, pour the water, milk, and stock cube and bring to a boil. Add the polenta, stir with a wooden spoon, and cook over medium heat for the time listed on the package, stirring occasionally.
2. When the polenta comes off the edge, add the cheese and stir with a wooden spoon to incorporate it. Season with salt and pepper and serve immediately.

*What the toddler can do:* dose the ingredients and grate the cheese.

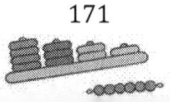

## 20. Baked Cod

*Preparation: 15 min | Cooking: 17 min | Servings: 4*
*Ingredients:*

- 2 cod fillets
- 2 cloves of garlic
- 2 lemons
- A few basil leaves
- 2 sprigs of cherry tomatoes
- Olive oil to taste.

*Directions:*

1. Preheat the oven to 350°F and line a baking sheet with baking paper. Arrange the cod fillets on the prepared baking sheet.
2. Wash the lemons and cut them into slices; wash the cherry tomatoes; peel and mince the garlic. Add the lemon slices, minced garlic, basil leaves, and cherry tomatoes to the baking dish. Season with a little salt and a drizzle of olive oil, and bake in the oven for about 17 minutes.

*What the toddler can do:* wash the vegetables, and arrange the ingredients in the pan.

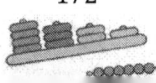

## 21. Mashed Potatoes

*Preparation: 20 min | Cooking: 60 min | Servings: 4*
*Ingredients:*

- 2 lb 4 oz yellow floury potatoes
- ¾ cup whole milk
- 1 oz butter
- 1 oz Parmesan cheese
- Fine salt to taste.
- Nutmeg to taste.

*Directions:*

1. Using a grater, grate the Parmesan cheese and set aside. Boil the potatoes for 35-40 minutes. If you insert a fork and notice they are soft, drain them and let them cool before peeling. Meanwhile, heat the milk in a small saucepan.
2. Mash the potatoes with a potato masher and place the pulp in a saucepan. Season with a pinch of salt and nutmeg. Pour in the hot milk and cook over low heat, stirring with a whisk until completely absorbed. Turn off the flame and add the butter, stirring well with a wooden spoon to cream, and finally add the grated Parmesan cheese.

*What the toddler can do:* grate the Parmesan cheese, mash the potatoes, and weigh and mix the ingredients.

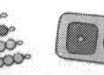

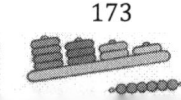

## 22. Turkey Meatballs

*Preparation: 10 min. | Cooking: 30 min. | Servings: 3-4*

*Ingredients:*

- 1 lb turkey mince
- 100g of ricotta cheese
- ½ glass of milk
- 1 egg (optional)
- 1 teaspoon salt
- Ginger and sweet paprika powder to taste.
- Extra virgin olive oil to taste.
- 1 clove of garlic
- Breadcrumbs to taste.

*Directions:*

1. Place the ground turkey, salt, ginger, paprika, milk, ricotta cheese, and egg in a bowl and mix with a fork. Add the breadcrumbs a little at a time and mix until the mixture is workable. Form the meatballs.
2. Heat a little oil and a clove of garlic in a frying pan. Add the meatballs and cook them over low heat for about 30 minutes. Serve the meatballs together with a side of vegetables.

*What the toddler can do:* dose and mix the ingredients and form the meatballs.

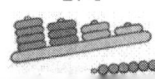

## 23. Stringy Spinach Meatballs

*Preparation: 10 min. | Cooking: 30 min. | Servings: 3*
*Ingredients:*

- 7 oz cooked and squeezed spinach
- 9 oz of ricotta cheese
- 1 egg
- ¾ oz grated Grana cheese
- 1 pinch of salt
- nutmeg
- 4 oz of breadcrumbs
- 4 oz mozzarella cheese for pizza

*Directions:*

1. Pour the ricotta into a bowl and mash it with a fork. Add the already cooked and well-squeezed spinach, egg, Grana cheese, a pinch of nutmeg, and salt and mix well until smooth. Add the breadcrumbs a little at a time while continuing to mix.
2. Dice the mozzarella cheese and place some on a flat plate with some bread crumbs. Take some of the dough with your hands and form small balls. Crush them to form a disc, put two or three cubes of mozzarella inside, and close forming the meatballs. Make 12 meatballs, coat them in breadcrumbs, and place them on an empty plate.
3. Preheat the oven to 375°F in fan mode. Grease a baking sheet with a little oil and then arrange the meatballs. Bake for 20 minutes, turning once halfway through cooking. Alternatively, you can fry the meatballs.

*What the toddler can do:* weigh and mix ingredients, crack the egg, grate cheese, and make meatballs.

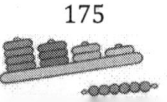

## 24. Savory Pancakes

*Preparation: 15 min. | Cooking: 30 min. | Servings: 3-4*

Ingredients:
- 2 eggs
- 2 teaspoons of sugar
- 1 teaspoon salt
- 3 tablespoons sunflower seed oil
- 1 cup milk
- 2 teaspoons baking powder
- 2 cups of 00 flour
- Frankfurters, carrots, olives, peas, peppers, tomatoes, etc.; for decoration

Directions:

1. Cook the ingredients for decoration and keep them aside.
2. In a bowl, crack eggs, add sugar and salt, and whisk with an electric mixer. Gradually add the milk, oil, and flour while continuing to whisk; finally, add the baking powder.
3. Grease a nonstick frying pan with a little oil or some butter and pour in a generous spoonful of batter. As soon as it starts to set, immediately create the eyes (for example, with two rounds of frankfurter or olives) and the mouth (with a slice of red bell pepper). Turn the pancake over and cook it on the other side for a couple of minutes.
4. Transfer the pancake to a plate and continue decorating it by making the nose, hair, and eyebrows. You can use half a cherry tomato for the nose and grated carrots or peas for the hair. Set your child's imagination free by letting him decorate his pancakes.

*What the toddler can do:* weigh and mix the ingredients, grate the carrots, break the egg, and decorate the pancakes.

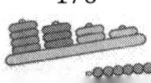

## 25. Pasta with Soft Cheese

*Preparation: 2 min | Cooking: 10 min | Servings: 1*
*Ingredients:*

- 2 oz pasta (pennette, farfalle or risoni)
- 1 soft cheese for children
- 1 tablespoon of pasta cooking water
- 1 tablespoon grated parmesan cheese

*Directions:*

1. In a small saucepan, boil water. Add salt and pour in the pasta. Meanwhile, in a dish, put the soft cheese, Parmesan cheese, and a tablespoon of the pasta cooking water and mix well. Drain the pasta and stir it into the dish along with the other ingredients.

*What the toddler can do:* Dose and mix the ingredients.

## 26. Baked Fish Cutlets

*Preparation: 2 min | Cooking: 10 min | Servings: 1*
*Ingredients:*

- 1 fish fillet of your choice
- 2 oz of breadcrumbs
- 1 tablespoon of grated parmesan cheese
- 1 sprig of parsley
- extra virgin olive oil to taste
- garlic (optional)

*Directions:*

1. Line a baking sheet with baking paper and preheat the oven to 350°F.
2. Remove the soul from the garlic and mince it very finely. Also, chop the parsley and grate the parmesan; put the breadcrumbs, parmesan, chopped parsley and garlic, and oil in a bowl and mix well.
3. Dip the fish fillets in the breadcrumbs and press well with your hands so that they stick together.
4. Arrange the fish fillets on top of the prepared baking dish and add the remaining breadcrumbs on top.
5. Drizzle the fish cutlets with a drizzle of extra virgin olive oil and bake in the oven for about 20 minutes. For extra crispiness, turn on the grill during the last 5 minutes of baking..

*What the toddler can do:* Dose and mix the ingredients and bread the fish.

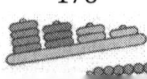

## 27. Pesto pasta

*Preparation: 15 min | Cooking: 10 min | Servings: 4*
*Ingredients:*

- 12 oz of pasta (pennette, farfalle, tortiglioni)
- 2½ oz basil
- ½ cup extra virgin olive oil
- 6 tablespoons of 36-month Parmesan cheese
- 2 tablespoons pecorino cheese
- 1 oz pine nuts
- 2 cloves of garlic
- 1 pinch of coarse salt

*Directions:*

1. Bring a pot of water to a boil. When it boils, add the salt and pasta and cook for the time indicated on the package.
2. Meanwhile, wash and dry the basil leaves and place them in the mortar along with the coarse salt. Pound with rotary motions, add the ingredients and continue pounding until creamy.
3. Drain the pasta, place it in a bowl, and toss it with plenty of pesto.

*What the toddler can do:* Dose the ingredients, and make pesto using the mortar and pestle.

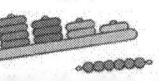

## 28. Baked Chicken Cutlets

*Preparation: 10 min | Cooking: 25 min | Servings: 4*

Ingredients:

- 4 slices Chicken breast (unbeaten)
- 200g of breadcrumbs
- 100g Parmesan cheese
- 1 clove of garlic
- Parsley to taste.
- ½ glass of extra virgin olive oil
- Salt to taste.
- Pepper to taste.
- Milk to taste.
- Flour q.b.
- 1 egg

Directions:

1. Preheat the oven to 400°F and line a baking sheet with baking paper.
2. Remove the soul from the garlic, chop it very finely, and place it in a bowl. Also, chop the parsley, grate the Parmesan cheese, and transfer them to the bowl; add the breadcrumbs, a pinch of salt, and the oil and mix well.
3. Let the chicken breast slices soak in milk for a few minutes. In another dish, beat the egg with a fork. Drain the chicken breast slices and coat them first in flour, then in the egg, and finally in the breadcrumbs, pressing well with your hands to make them stick. Arrange the cutlets on the prepared baking sheet, drizzle with a little olive oil, and bake in the oven for 25 minutes until they reach the desired crispness.

*What the toddler can do:* dose and mix ingredients, break the egg, and bread the chicken.

## 29. Vegetable Meatballs

Preparation: 15 min | Cooking: 45 min | Servings: 4

Ingredients:

- 1 lb of zucchini
- 7 oz of carrots
- 3 tablespoons of Parmigiano Reggiano DOP
- 2 oz of bread
- Milk to taste.
- 1 egg
- extra virgin olive oil q.b.

Directions:

1. Wash the zucchini, peel the carrots, and remove both ends. Steam the vegetables with a cup of water for about 25 minutes. When they are soft, drain them, cut them into pieces, and squeeze them. Transfer the vegetables to a bowl.
2. Wet the bread with milk and squeeze it very well before adding it to the bowl with the vegetables. Add the egg, grated Parmesan cheese, and a pinch of salt and mix well with your hands until smooth. Form into patties, or you can form burgers by taking more dough and crushing it into a disc.
3. Heat a nonstick skillet with a tiny bit of extra virgin olive oil and cook the patties or burgers for 10 minutes per side until they form a crust.

*What the toddler can do:* weigh and mix ingredients, crack the egg, grate cheese, and make meatballs.

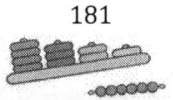

## 30. Sausage and Baked Potatoes

*Preparation: 10 min | Cooking: 45 min | Servings: 4*

*Ingredients:*

- 2 lb of sausage
- 1 lb of potatoes
- 2 cloves of garlic without a soul
- 3 tablespoons of breadcrumbs
- 2 sprigs of rosemary
- A pinch of salt

*Directions:*

1. Preheat the oven to 400°F.
2. Peel the potatoes and cut them into wedges or pieces that are not too large.
3. Cut the sausage into pieces and put it in a bowl along with the potatoes, garlic cloves, salt, rosemary, and bread crumbs. Mix everything so that the flavors are blended. Transfer the contents of the bowl to a baking dish and bake in the oven for about 45 minutes, stirring once halfway through cooking. You can set the grill mode for the last 5 minutes for best results.

**What the toddler can do:** peel the potatoes, and weigh and mix the ingredients.

## 31. Yogurt and Chocolate Chip Muffins

*Preparation: 10 min | Cooking: 20 min | Servings: 12*

*Ingredients:*

- 2 eggs
- ½ cup sugar
- ¼ cup sunflower oil
- ¼ cup milk
- ½ cup white yogurt
- 1 ¾ cup flour
- ½ oz baking powder (8g)
- 2½ oz of chocolate chips

*Directions:*

1. Place 12 paper ramekins in a muffin mold and preheat the oven to 375°F in static mode or 350°F in ventilated mode.
2. In a bowl, break the eggs and whisk them with an electric mixer. Gradually add the sugar, oil, milk, and yogurt jar. Add the flour and baking powder and continue mixing. Finally, add the chocolate chips to the mixture and mix with a spoon.
3. Pour the batter into the ramekins, filling them no more than ¾ full, and bake for 20 minutes. When they are golden brown on the surface, remove the muffins from the oven and let them cool. After that remove After that, remove them with a wooden stick and serve.

*What the toddler can do:* Dose and mix the ingredients, break the eggs, and pour the batter into the ramekins.

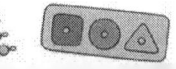

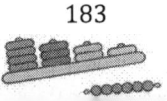

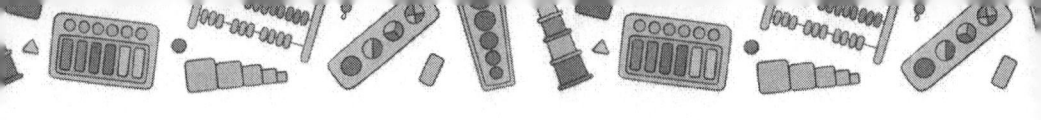

## 32. Shortbread Cookies without Butter

*Preparation: 10 min | Cooking: 15 min | Servings: 6*

*Ingredients:*

- Shortcrust pastry without butter
- Hazelnut cream, jam, or powdered sugar.

*Directions:*

1. Preheat the oven to 350°F and line a baking sheet with baking paper.
2. Roll out the dough with a rolling pin and cut out small disks using a pastry cup or glass Place some hazelnut cream in the center and close on itself, forming a small ball. Alternatively, you can make flower shapes with two different-sized molds.
3. Place the cookies on the prepared baking sheet and bake in the oven for 15 minutes.
4. If you made the filled cookies, you can dust them with powdered sugar; if you made the flowers, put a little jam on each large flower and rest the small flowers on top.

*What the toddler can do:* Stuff the cookies and arrange them on the baking sheet, and dust them with powdered sugar.

## 33. Daisy Cake

Preparation: 20 min | Cooking: 30 min | Servings: 6
Ingredients:

- 1 cup of 00 flour
- 1 cup of potato starch
- ½ cup sugar
- 2 oz butter or 3 tablespoons seed oil
- 3 Eggs
- 3 Yolks
- 1 Lemon peel
- Icing sugar to taste

Directions:

1. If you use butter, melt it and let it cool completely.
2. Preheat the oven to 325°F in fan mode, and butter and flour a 22-cm-diameter cake pan (or grease it with release spray).
3. Place the three whole eggs in a bowl, add the sugar, and beat with electric whips for about 10 minutes until whitish and fluffy. At this point, add the yolks and continue whipping for another 10 minutes.
4. Add the grated lemon zest, sift the 00 flour and potato starch, and gently add them to the mixture, gradually incorporating them with a pastry spatula in slow movements from the bottom to the top. Now add the melted butter or seed oil and incorporate it without disassembling the mixture.
5. Pour the batter into the cake pan and level the surface. Bake for about 35 minutes (insert a toothpick to see if it is fully cooked inside; if it comes out clean, it is cooked). Turn off the oven and let the cake cool inside with the open door. Before serving, take the daisy cake out of the oven and dust it with powdered sugar.

*What the toddler can do:* weigh and mix the ingredients, crack open the eggs, butter the pan, and dust icing sugar.

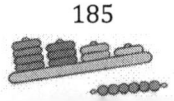

# Conclusions

We have thus concluded our guide. I hope that it may help you stimulate your baby's mind and follow his development so that day by day, he becomes more and more responsible, independent, and able to make his own decisions.

We looked at the principles behind the famous Montessori Method, saw how the toddler improves his sensory abilities and skills at different stages of development and examined his needs at different age groups. We have also considered the role of the adult, particularly that of the parent, to see what kind of position they must play in the toddler's life and how they can meet the toddler's needs without resorting to punishment and reproach.

We then approached the practical side by first trying to figure out how to organize the different rooms in the house while always respecting the principles of the Montessori Method until we got to the different stimulation, hands-on living, sensory and developmental activities divided by age group. Finally, we proposed some fun outdoor activities and concluded our guide with more than 30 tasty recipes to make with your toddler to engage them and further develop their senses and skills.

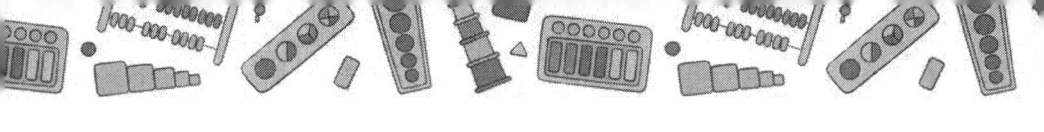

In conclusion, we can say that the Montessori Method is not just an educational method and has nothing to do with school education systems. It is a true way of life that prepares each child to be a responsible adult by challenging their limitations to be the best version of themselves.

At this point, you have all the tools you need to unleash your child's potential and foster his development positively and constructively! Help him to do it himself! Allow him to experience his surroundings, work with his hands, and learn from his mistakes. Only in this way will you raise a responsible adult, confident in himself and his abilities and sensitive to others and other forms of life.

We cannot leave without first meditating on a beautiful reflection by our guide's muse, Maria Montessori:

*"Through this experience of the 'environment,' in the form of play, he [the child] examines the things and impressions he has received in his unconscious mind. Using the work he becomes conscious and builds the 'Man.' The child is directed by a mysterious, marvelously great power, which little by little he embodies; he thus becomes a man and becomes a man using his hands, through his experience: first through play and then through work. Hands are the instrument of human intelligence. By these experiences, the child takes on a definite and therefore*

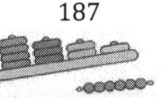

*limited form, since awareness is always more limited than 'unconsciousness and subconsciousness.'"* [27]

Moms and Dads, give dignity to your children, treat them with respect, and above all, never stop defending their rights, especially the right to freedom!

I hope this book has been helpful to you and will be your companion as you follow your toddlers as they grow.

Did you enjoy the book?

I hope so!

I work hard to provide quality content, but *I need your help to grow*. Your input makes a difference; it is *very important* to me!

Please, if you found this book useful and liked it, leave a review on Amazon, *I will appreciate it very much*. With your help, I will be able to increase the book's visibility and *help many more people*.

Thank you from the bottom of my heart!

*Serena De Micheli*

---

[27] M. MONTESSORI, *La mente del bambino*, Garzanti, Milan, 1952, 27.

# Bibliography

LILLARD A.S., *Montessori: The science behind the genius*, New York, Oxford University Press, 2005.

MONTESSORI M., *Formazione dell'uomo*, Garzanti, Milan, 1949.

MONTESSORI M., *Il Metodo della Pedagogia Scientifica applicato all'educazione infantile nelle Case dei Bambini*, Edizioni Opera Nazionale Montessori, Rome, 2000.

MONTESSORI M., *Il segreto dell'infanzia*, Garzanti, Milan, 1950.

MONTESSORI M., *La mente del bambino*, Garzanti, Milan, 1952.

MONTESSORI M., *La scoperta del bambino*, Garzanti, Milan, 1970.

MONTESSORI M., *Educare alla libertà*, Laterza, Bari, 1950.

MONTESSORI M., *Educazione e pace*, Opera Nazionale Montessori, Rome, 2004.

# Sitography

BIJNENS E.M. - DEROM C. – THIERY E. WEYERS S. – NAWROT T.S., *Residential green space and child intelligence and behavior across urban, suburban, and rural areas in Belgium: A longitudinal birth cohort study of twins*, Plos Medicine, 18 August 2020, in https://journals.plos.org/plosmedicine/article?id=10.1371/journal.pmed.1003213.

LILLARD A.S. - ELSE N. - QUEST, *The early years: evaluating Montessori Method*, Science, (2006), 313, 1893 in http://www.sciencemag.org/cgi/content/full/313/5795/1893.

METODO MONTESSORI, in https://www.metodomontessori.it/.

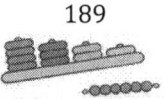

Printed in Great Britain
by Amazon